# Your Office

## Getting Started with Microsoft® SharePoint® 2013

D1403858

## Amy Kinser

ERIC J. SCHMIEDER

PEARSON

Boston  Columbus  Indianapolis  New York  San Francisco  Upper Saddle River
Amsterdam  Cape Town  Dubai  London  Madrid  Milan  Munich  Paris  Montréal  Toronto
Delhi  Mexico City  São Paulo  Sydney  Hong Kong  Seoul  Singapore  Taipei  Tokyo

**VP of Career Skills:** Andrew Gilfillan
**Senior Editor:** Samantha McAfee Lewis
**Team Lead, Project Management:** Laura Burgess
**Project Manager:** Anne Garcia
**Program Manager:** Natacha Moore
**Development Editor:** Nancy Lamm, N. Lamm Consulting Associates, Ltd.
**Editorial Assistant:** Victoria Lasavath
**Director of Product Marketing:** Maggie Waples
**Director of Field Marketing:** Leigh Ann Sims
**Field Marketing Managers:** Brad Forrester & Joanna Sabella

**Marketing Coordinator:** Susan Osterlitz
**Senior Operations Specialist:** Maura Zaldivar
**Senior Art Director:** Diane Ernsberger
**Interior and Cover Design:** Diane Ernsberger
**Associate Director of Design:** Blair Brown
**Digital Media Editor:** Eric Hakanson
**Director of Media Development:** Taylor Ragan
**Media Project Manager, Production:** John Cassar
**Full-Service Project Management:** GEX Publishing Services
**Composition:** GEX Publishing Services

Credits and acknowledgments borrowed from other sources and reproduced, with permission, in this textbook appear on the appropriate page within text.

**Library of Congress Control Number:** 2014940102

10 9 8 7 6 5 4 3 2 1
ISBN-13: 978-0-13-334868-2
ISBN-10: 0-13-334868-7

# About the Authors

## Amy S. Kinser, Esq., Series Editor

Amy holds a B.A. degree in Chemistry with a Business minor from Indiana University, and a J.D. from the Maurer School of Law, also at Indiana University. After working as an environmental chemist, starting her own technology consulting company, and practicing intellectual property law, she has spent the past 12 years teaching technology at the Kelley School of Business in Bloomington, Indiana—#1 ranked school for undergraduate program performance in the specialty of Information Systems according to 2012 Bloomberg Businessweek. Currently, she serves as the Director of Computer Skills and Senior Lecturer at the Kelley School of Business at Indiana University. She also loves spending time with her two sons, Aidan and J. Matthew, and her husband J. Eric.

*I dedicate this series to my Kinser Boyz for their unwavering love, support, and patience; to my family; to my students for inspiring me; to Sam for believing in me; and to the instructors. I hope this series will inspire!*
**Amy Kinser**

## Eric J. Schmieder

Eric holds a Masters in Entrepreneurship and a B.S.B.A. in Computer Information Systems with a minor in Mathematics, both from Western Carolina University. He is a candidate for a Ph.D. in Technology Management with a focus in Digital Communication Systems from Indiana State University. He is a full time Computer Technology Faculty member at Johnston Community College in Smithfield, NC; has over a decade of experience as a small business owner and entrepreneur, providing real-world technology solutions on Microsoft platforms; and is an adjunct instructor with North Carolina State University and several colleges in the North Carolina Community College System. He has a passion for teaching while remaining current in the technology industry. This is Eric's second book in the *Your Office* series, having also written, *Your Office: Getting Started with Microsoft Office 365.*

*I dedicate this book to my loving wife, Crissy, and our two children, Noah and Serenity, who have selflessly provided me the time needed to complete the writing of this book; to my family and friends that have cheered me in these efforts; to Amy, Sam, Anne, and Nancy who have encouraged and helped me every step of the way; to my work family at JCC and BRCC and all of my students who continue to give me opportunity to learn and to share my knowledge of computers with them.*
**Eric Schmieder**

# Contents

# Acknowledgments

The *Your Office* team would like to thank the following reviewers who have invested time and energy to help shape this series from the very beginning, providing us with invaluable feedback through their comments, suggestions, and constructive criticism.

We'd like to especially thank our Focus Group attendees and User Diary Reviewers:

**Heather Albinger**
Waukesha County Technical College

**Melody Alexander**
Ball State University

**Mazhar Anik**
Owens Community College

**David Antol**
Hartford Community College

**Cheryl Brown**
Delgado Community College

**Janet Campbell**
Dixie State College

**Kuan Chen**
Purdue Calumet

**Jennifer Day**
Sinclair Community College

**Joseph F. Domagala**
Duquesne University

**Christa Fairman**
Arizona Western University

**Denise Farley**
Sussex County Community College

**Drew Foster**
Miami University of Ohio

**Lorie Goodgine**
Tennessee Technology Center in Paris

**Jane L. Hammer**
Valley City State University

**Kay Johnson**
Community College of Rhode Island

**Susumu Kasai**
Salt Lake Community College

**Linda Kavanaugh**
Robert Morris University

**Jennifer Krou**
Texas State University, San Marcos

**Michelle Mallon**
Ohio State University

**Sandra McCormack**
Monroe Community College

**Melissa Nemeth**
Indiana University – Purdue University, Indianapolis

**Janet Olfert**
North Dakota State University

**Patsy Ann Parker**
Southwestern Oklahoma State University

**Cheryl Reindl-Johnson**
Sinclair Community College

**Jennifer Robinson**
Trident Technical College

**Tony Rose**
Miami University of Ohio

**Cindi Smatt**
North Georgia College & State University

**Jenny Lee Svelund**
University of Utah

**William VanderClock**
Bentley University

**Jill Weiss**
Florida International University

**Lin Zhao**
Purdue Calumet

We'd like to thank all of our conscientious reviewers, including those who contributed to our previous editions:

**Sven Aelterman**
Troy University

**Nitin Aggarwal**
San Jose State University

**Angel Alexander**
Piedmont Technical College

**Melody Alexander**
Ball State University

**Karen Allen**
Community College of Rhode Island

**Maureen Allen**
Elon University

**Wilma Andrews**
Virginia Commonwealth University

**Mazhar Anik**
Owens Community College

**David Antol**
Harford Community College

**Kirk Atkinson**
Western Kentucky University

**Barbara Baker**
Indiana Wesleyan University

**Kristi Berg**
Minot State University

**Kavuri Bharath**
Old Dominion University

**Ann Blackman**
Parkland College

**Jeanann Boyce**
Montgomery College

**Lynn Brooks**
Tyler Junior College

**Cheryl Brown**
Delgado Community College, West Bank Campus

**Bonnie Buchanan**
Central Ohio Technical College

**Peggy Burrus**
Red Rocks Community College

**Richard Cacace**
Pensacola State College

**Margo Chaney**
Carroll Community College

**Shanan Chappell**
College of the Albemarle, North Carolina

**Kuan Chen**
Purdue Calumet

**David Childress**
Ashland Community and Technical College

**Keh-Wen Chuang**
Purdue University, North Central

**Suzanne Clayton**
Drake University

**Amy Clubb**
Portland Community College

**Bruce Collins**
Davenport University

**Margaret Cooksey**
Tallahassee Community College

**Charmayne Cullom**
University of Northern Colorado

**Christy Culver**
Marion Technical College

**Juliana Cypert**
Tarrant County College

**Harold Davis**
Southeastern Louisiana University

**Jeff Davis**
Jamestown Community College

**Jennifer Day**
Sinclair Community College

**Anna Degtyareva**
Mt. San Antonio College

**Beth Deinert**
Southeast Community College

**Kathleen DeNisco**
Erie Community College

**Donald Dershem**
Mountain View College

**Bambi Edwards**
Craven Community College

**Elaine Emanuel**
Mt. San Antonio College

**Diane Endres**
Ancilla College

**Nancy Evans**
Indiana University – Purdue University,
Indianapolis

**Christa Fairman**
Arizona Western College

**Marni Ferner**
University of North Carolina, Wilmington

**Paula Fisher**
Central New Mexico Community College

**Linda Fried**
University of Colorado, Denver

**Diana Friedman**
Riverside Community College

**Susan Fry**
Boise State University

**Virginia Fullwood**
Texas A&M University, Commerce

**Janos Fustos**
Metropolitan State College of Denver

**John Fyfe**
University of Illinois at Chicago

**Saiid Ganjalizadeh**
The Catholic University of America

**Randolph Garvin**
Tyler Junior College

**Diane Glowacki**
Tarrant County College

**Jerome Gonnella**
Northern Kentucky University

**Connie Grimes**
Morehead State University

**Debbie Gross**
Ohio State University

**Babita Gupta**
California State University,
Monterey Bay

**Lewis Hall**
Riverside City College

**Jane Hammer**
Valley City State University

**Marie Hartlein**
Montgomery County Community College

**Darren Hayes**
Pace University

**Paul Hayes**
Eastern New Mexico University

**Mary Hedberg**
Johnson County Community College

**Lynda Henrie**
LDS Business College

**Deedee Herrera**
Dodge City Community College

**Marilyn Hibbert**
Salt Lake Community College

**Jan Hime**
University of Nebraska, Lincoln

**Cheryl Hinds**
Norfolk State University

**Mary Kay Hinkson**
Fox Valley Technical College

**Margaret Hohly**
Cerritos College

**Brian Holbert**
Spring Hill College

**Susan Holland**
Southeast Community College

**Anita Hollander**
University of Tennessee, Knoxville

**Emily Holliday**
Campbell University

**Stacy Hollins**
St. Louis Community College,
Florissant Valley

**Mike Horn**
State University of New York, Geneseo

**Christie Hovey**
Lincoln Land Community College

**Margaret Hvatum**
St. Louis Community College, Meramec

**Jean Insinga**
Middlesex Community College

**Jon (Sean) Jasperson**
Texas A&M University

**Glen Jenewein**
Kaplan University

**Gina Jerry**
Santa Monica College

**Dana Johnson**
North Dakota State University

**Mary Johnson**
Mt. San Antonio College

**Linda Johnsonius**
Murray State University

**Carla Jones**
Middle Tennessee State University

**Susan Jones**
Utah State University

**Nenad Jukic**
Loyola University, Chicago

**Sali Kaceli**
Philadelphia Biblical University

**Sue Kanda**
Baker College of Auburn Hills

**Robert Kansa**
Macomb Community College

**Susumu Kasai**
Salt Lake Community College

**Linda Kavanaugh**
Robert Morris University

**Debby Keen**
University of Kentucky

**Mike Kelly**
Community College of Rhode Island

**Melody Kiang**
California State University, Long Beach

**Lori Kielty**
College of Central Florida

**Richard Kirk**
Pensacola State College

**Dawn Konicek**
Blackhawk Tech

**John Kucharczuk**
Centennial College

**David Largent**
Ball State University

**Frank Lee**
Fairmont State University

**Luis Leon**
The University of Tennessee at Chattanooga

**Freda Leonard**
Delgado Community College

**Julie Lewis**
Baker College, Allen Park

**Suhong Li**
Bryant University

**Renee Lightner**
Florida State College

**John Lombardi**
South University

**Rhonda Lucas**
Spring Hill College

**Adriana Lumpkin**
Midland College

**Lynne Lyon**
Durham College

**Nicole Lytle**
California State University,
San Bernardino

**Donna Madsen**
Kirkwood Community College

**Susan Maggio**
Community College of Baltimore County

**Kim Manning**
Tallahassee Community College

**Paul Martin**
Harrisburg Area Community College

**Cheryl Martucci**
Diablo Valley College

**Sebena Masline**
Florida State College of Jacksonville

**Sherry Massoni**
Harford Community College

**Lee McClain**
Western Washington University

**Sandra McCormack**
Monroe Community College

**Sue McCrory**
Missouri State University

**Barbara Miller**
University of Notre Dame

**Michael O. Moorman**
Saint Leo University

**Kathleen Morris**
University of Alabama

**Alysse Morton**
Westminster College

**Elobaid Muna**
University of Maryland Eastern Shore

**Jackie Myers**
Sinclair Community College

**Russell Myers**
El Paso Community College

**Bernie Negrete**
Cerritos College

**Melissa Nemeth**
Indiana University – Purdue University,
Indianapolis

**Jennifer Nightingale**
Duquesne University

**Kathie O'Brien**
North Idaho College

**Michael Ogawa**
University of Hawaii

**Rene Pack**
Arizona Western College

**Patsy Parker**
Southwest Oklahoma State University

**Laurie Patterson**
University of North Carolina, Wilmington

**Alicia Pearlman**
Baker College

**Diane Perreault**
Sierra College and California State University,
Sacramento

**Theresa Phinney**
Texas A&M University

**Vickie Pickett**
Midland College

**Marcia Polanis**
Forsyth Technical Community College

**Rose Pollard**
Southeast Community College

**Stephen Pomeroy**
Norwich University

**Leonard Presby**
William Paterson University

**Donna Reavis**
Delta Career Education

**Eris Reddoch**
Pensacola State College

**James Reddoch**
Pensacola State College

**Michael Redmond**
La Salle University

**Terri Rentfro**
John A. Logan College

**Vicki Robertson**
Southwest Tennessee Community College

**Dianne Ross**
University of Louisiana at Lafayette

**Ann Rowlette**
Liberty University

**Amy Rutledge**
Oakland University

**Candace Ryder**
Colorado State University

**Joann Segovia**
Winona State University

**Eileen Shifflett**
James Madison University

**Sandeep Shiva**
Old Dominion University

**Robert Sindt**
Johnson County Community College

**Cindi Smatt**
Texas A&M University

**Edward Souza**
Hawaii Pacific University

**Nora Spencer**
Fullerton College

**Alicia Stonesifer**
La Salle University

**Cheryl Sypniewski**
Macomb Community College

**Arta Szathmary**
Bucks County Community College

**Nasser Tadayon**
Southern Utah University

**Asela Thomason**
California State University Long Beach

**Nicole Thompson**
Carteret Community College

**Terri Tiedema**
Southeast Community College, Nebraska

**Lewis Todd**
Belhaven University

**Barb Tollinger**
Sinclair Community College

**Allen Truell**
Ball State University

**Erhan Uskup**
Houston Community College

**Lucia Vanderpool**
Baptist College of Health Sciences

**Michelle Vlaich-Lee**
Greenville Technical College

**Barry Walker**
Monroe Community College

**Rosalyn Warren**
Enterprise State Community College

**Sonia Washington**
Prince George's Community College

**Eric Weinstein**
Suffolk County Community College

**Jill Weiss**
Florida International University

**Lorna Wells**
Salt Lake Community College

**Rosalie Westerberg**
Clover Park Technical College

**Clemetee Whaley**
Southwest Tennessee Community College

**Kenneth Whitten**
Florida State College of Jacksonville

**MaryLou Wilson**
Piedmont Technical College

**John Windsor**
University of North Texas

**Kathy Winters**
University of Tennessee, Chattanooga

**Nancy Woolridge**
Fullerton College

**Jensen Zhao**
Ball State University

**Martha Zimmer**
University of Evansville

**Molly Zimmer**
University of Evansville

**Mary Anne Zlotow**
College of DuPage

**Matthew Zullo**
Wake Technical Community College

Additionally, we'd like to thank our MyITLab team for their review and collaboration with our text authors:

**LeeAnn Bates**

**Jennifer Hurley**

**Ralph Moore**

**Jerri Williams**

**Jaimie Noy**
Media Producer

# Preface

The *Your Office* series focuses first and foremost on preparing students to use both technical and soft skills in the real world. Our goal is to provide this to both instructors and students through a modern approach to teaching and learning Microsoft Office applications, an approach that weaves in the technical content using a realistic business scenario and focuses on using Office as a decision-making tool.

The process of developing this unique series for you, the modern student or instructor, requires innovative ideas regarding the pedagogy and organization of the text. You learn best when doing—so you will be active from Page 1. Your learning goes to the next level when you are challenged to do more with less—your hand will be held at first but, progressively, the case exercises require more from you. Because you care about how things work in the real world—in your classes, your future jobs, your personal life—Real World Advice, Videos, and Success Stories are woven throughout the text. These innovative features will help you progress from a basic understanding of Office to mastery of each application, empowering you to perform with confidence in Windows 8, Word, Excel, Access, and PowerPoint, including on mobile devices.

No matter what career you may choose to pursue in life, this series will give you the foundation to succeed. *Your Office* uses cases that will enable you to be immersed in a realistic business as you learn Office in the context of a running business scenario—the Painted Paradise Resort & Spa. You will immediately delve into the many interesting, smaller businesses in this resort (golf course, spa, restaurants, hotel, etc.) to learn how a larger organization actually uses Office. You will learn how to make Office work for you now, as a student, and in your future career.

Today, the experience of working with Office is not isolated to working in a job in a cubicle. Your physical office is wherever you are with a laptop or a mobile device. Office has changed. It's modern. It's mobile. It's personal. And when you learn these valuable skills and master Office, you are able to make Office your own. The title of this series is a promise to you, the student: Our goal is to make Microsoft Office *Your Office*.

# Key Features

- **Starting and Ending Files:** These appear before every case in the text. Starting Files identify exactly which Student Data Files are needed to complete each case. Ending Files are provided to show students the naming conventions they should use when saving their files. Each file icon is color coded by application.

- **Workshop Objectives List:** The learning objectives to be achieved as students work through the workshop. Page numbers are included for easy reference. These are revisited in the Concept Check at the end of the workshop.

- **Real World Success:** A boxed feature in the workshop opener that shares an anecdote from a real former student, describing how knowledge of Office has helped him or her to get ahead or be successful in his or her life.

- **Active Text Box:** Represents the active portion of the workshop and is easily distinguishable from explanatory text by the blue shaded background. Active Text helps students quickly identify what steps they need to follow to complete the workshop Prepare Case.

- **Quick Reference Box:** A boxed feature in the workshop, summarizing generic or alternative instructions on how to accomplish a task. This feature enables students to quickly find important skills.

- **Real World Advice Box:** A boxed feature in the workshop, offering advice and best practices for general use of important Office skills. The goal is to advise students as a manager might in a future job.

- **Side Note:** A brief tip or piece of information aligned visually with a step in the workshop, quickly providing key information to students completing that particular step.

- **Consider This:** In-text critical thinking questions and topics for discussion, set apart as a boxed feature, allowing students to step back from the project and think about the application of what they are learning and how these concepts might be used in the future.

- **Concept Check:** Review questions appearing at the end of the workshop, which require students to demonstrate their understanding of the objectives in that workshop.

- **Visual Summary:** A visual review of the objectives learned in the workshop using images from the completed solution file, mapped to the workshop objectives using callouts and page references so students can easily find the section of text to refer to for a refresher.

- **Business Application Icons:** Appear with every case in the text and clearly identify which business application students are being exposed to, i.e., Finance, Marketing, Operations, etc.

## Business Application Icons

Customer
Service

Finance &
Accounting

General
Business

Human
Resources

Information
Technology

Production &
Operations

Sales &
Marketing

Research &
Development

# Instructor Resources

The Instructor's Resource Center, available at www.pearsonhighered.com, includes the following:

- Prepared Exams with solution files for additional assessment.
- Annotated Solution Files with Scorecards assist with grading the Prepare, Practice, Problem Solve, and Perform Cases.
- Data and Solution Files.
- Rubrics for Perform Cases in Microsoft Word format enable instructors to easily grade open-ended assignments with no definite solution.
- PowerPoint Presentations with notes for each chapter.
- Instructor's Manual that provides detailed blueprints to achieve workshop learning objectives and outcomes and best use the unique structure of the modules.
- Complete Test Bank, also available in TestGen format.
- Syllabus templates.
- Additional Practice, Problem Solve, and Perform Cases to provide you with variety and choice in exercises both on the workshop and module levels.
- Scripted Lectures provide instructors with a lecture outline that mirrors the Workshop Prepare Case.
- Flexible, robust, and customizable content is available for all major online course platforms that include everything instructors need in one place. Please contact your sales representative for information on accessing course cartridges for WebCT or Blackboard.

# Student Resources

- Companion Website
- Student Data Files

# Pearson's Companion Website

www.pearsonhighered.com/youroffice offers expanded IT resources and downloadable supplements. Students can find the following self-study tools for each workshop:

- Online Workshop Review
- Workshop Objectives
- Glossary
- Student Data Files

Dear Students,

If you want an edge over the competition, make it personal. Whether you love sports, travel, the stock market, or ballet, your passion is personal to you. Capitalizing on your passion leads to success. You live in a global marketplace, and your competition is global. The honors students in China exceed the total number of students in North America. Skills can help set you apart, but passion will make you stand above. *Your Office* is the tool to harness your passion's true potential.

In prior generations, personalization in a professional setting was discouraged. You had a "work" life and a "home" life. As the Series Editor, I write to you about the vision for *Your Office* from my laptop, on my couch, in the middle of the night when inspiration strikes me. My classroom and living room are my office. Life has changed from generations before us.

So, let's get personal. My degrees are not in technology, but chemistry and law. I helped put myself through school by working full time in various jobs, including a successful technology consulting business that continues today. My generation did not grow up with computers, but I did. My father was a network administrator for the military. So, I was learning to program in Basic before anyone had played Nintendo's Duck Hunt or Tetris. Technology has always been one of my passions from a young age. In fact, I now tell my husband: don't buy me jewelry for my birthday, buy me the latest gadget on the market!

In my first law position, I was known as the Office guru to the extent that no one gave me a law assignment for the first two months. Once I submitted the assignment, my supervisor remarked, "Wow, you don't just know how to leverage technology, but you really know the law too." I can tell you novel-sized stories from countless prior students in countless industries who gained an edge from using Office as a tool. Bringing technology to your passion makes you well-rounded and a cut above the rest, no matter the industry or position.

I am most passionate about teaching, in particular teaching technology. I come from many generations of teachers, including my mother who is a kindergarten teacher. For over 12 years, I have found my dream job passing on my passion for teaching, technology, law, science, music, and life in general at the Kelley School of Business at Indiana University. I have tried to pass on the key to engaging passion to my students. I have helped them see what differentiates them from all the other bright students vying for the same jobs.

Microsoft Office is a tool. All of your competition will have learned Microsoft Office to some degree or another. Some will have learned it to an advanced level. Knowing Microsoft Office is important, but it is also fundamental. Without it, you will not be considered for a position.

Today, you step into your first of many future roles bringing Microsoft Office to your dream job working for Painted Paradise Resort & Spa. You will delve into the business side of the resort and learn how to use *Your Office* to maximum benefit.

Don't let the context of a business fool you. If you don't think of yourself as a business person, you have no need to worry. Whether you realize it or not, everything is business. If you want to be a nurse, you are entering the health care industry. If you want to be a football player in the NFL, you are entering the business of sports as entertainment. In fact, if you want to be a stay-at-home parent, you are entering the business of a family household where *Your Office* still gives you an advantage. For example, you will be able to prepare a budget in Excel and analyze what you need to do to afford a trip to Disney World!

At Painted Paradise Resort & Spa, you will learn how to make Office yours through four learning levels designed to maximize your understanding. You will Prepare, Practice, and Problem Solve your tasks. Then, you will astound when you Perform your new talents. You will be challenged through Consider This questions and gain insight through Real World Advice.

There is something more. You want success in what you are passionate about in your life. It is personal for you. In this position at Painted Paradise Resort & Spa, you will gain your personal competitive advantage that will stay with you for the rest of your life—*Your Office*.

Sincerely,

*Amy Kinser*

*Series Editor*

Red Bluff Golf Course & Pro Shop

Turquoise Oasis Spa

Painted Treasures Gift Shop

Silver Moon Lounge

Event Planning & Catering

Indigo5 Restaurant

## Welcome to the Team!

Welcome to your new office at Painted Paradise Resort & Spa, where we specialize in painting perfect getaways. As the Chief Technology Officer, I am excited to have staff dedicated to the Microsoft Office integration between all the areas of the resort. Our team is passionate about our paradise, and I hope you find this to be your dream position here!

Painted Paradise is a resort and spa in New Mexico catering to business people, romantics, families, and anyone who just needs to get away. Inside our resort are many distinct areas. Many of these areas operate as businesses in their own right but must integrate with the other areas of the resort. The main areas of the resort are as follows.

- The **Hotel** is overseen by our Chief Executive Officer, William Mattingly, and is at the core of our business. The hotel offers a variety of accommodations, ranging from individual rooms to a grand villa suite. Further, the hotel offers packages including spa, golf, and special events.

  Room rates vary according to size, season, demand, and discount. The hotel has discounts for typical groups, such as AARP. The hotel also has a loyalty program where guests can earn free nights based on frequency of visits. Guests may charge anything from the resort to the room.

- **Red Bluff Golf Course** is a private world-class golf course and pro shop. The golf course has services such as golf lessons from the famous golf pro John Schilling and playing packages. Also, the golf course attracts local residents. This requires variety in pricing schemes to accommodate both local and hotel guests. The pro shop sells many retail items online.

  The golf course can also be reserved for special events and tournaments. These special events can be in conjunction with a wedding, conference, meetings, or other event covered by the event planning and catering area of the resort.

- **Turquoise Oasis Spa** is a full-service spa. Spa services include haircuts, pedicures, massages, facials, body wraps, waxing, and various other spa services—typical to exotic. Further, the spa offers private consultation, weight training (in the fitness center), a water bar, meditation areas, and steam rooms. Spa services are offered both in the spa and in the resort guest's room.

  Turquoise Oasis Spa uses top-of-the-line products and some house-brand products. The retail side offers products ranging from candles to age-defying home treatments. These products can also be purchased online. Many of the hotel guests who fall in love with the house-brand soaps, lotions, candles, and other items appreciate being able to buy more at any time.

  The spa offers a multitude of packages including special hotel room packages that include spa treatments. Local residents also use the spa. So, the spa guests are not limited to hotel guests. Thus, the packages also include pricing attractive to the local community.

---

- **Painted Treasures Gift Shop** has an array of items available for purchase, from toiletries to clothes to presents for loved ones back home including a healthy section of kids' toys for traveling business people. The gift shop sells a small sampling from the spa, golf course pro shop, and local New Mexico culture. The gift shop also has a small section of snacks and drinks. The gift shop has numerous part-time employees including students from the local college.

- **The Event Planning & Catering** area is central to attracting customers to the resort. From weddings to conferences, the resort is a popular destination. The resort has a substantial number of staff dedicated to planning, coordinating, setting up, catering, and maintaining these events. The resort has several facilities that can accommodate large groups. Packages and prices vary by size, room, and other services such as catering. Further, the Event Planning & Catering team works closely with local vendors for floral decorations, photography, and other event or wedding typical needs. However, all catering must go through the resort (no outside catering permitted). Lastly, the resort stocks several choices of decorations, table arrangements, and centerpieces. These range from professional, simple, themed, and luxurious.

- **Indigo5** and the **Silver Moon Lounge**, a world-class restaurant and lounge that is overseen by the well-known Chef Robin Sanchez. The cuisine is balanced and modern. From steaks to pasta to local southwestern meals, Indigo5 attracts local patrons in addition to resort guests. While the catering function is separate from the restaurant—though menu items may be shared—the restaurant does support all room service for the resort. The resort also has smaller food venues onsite such as the Terra Cotta Brew coffee shop in the lobby.

Currently, these areas are using Office to various degrees. In some areas, paper and pencil are still used for most business functions. Others have been lucky enough to have some technology savvy team members start Microsoft Office Solutions.

Using your skills, I am confident that you can help us integrate and use Microsoft Office on a whole new level! I hope you are excited to call Painted Paradise Resort & Spa *Your Office*.

Looking forward to working with you more closely!

*Aidan Matthews*

Aidan Matthews
Chief Technology Officer

## WORKSHOP 1 | BUILD A CORPORATE SITE COLLECTION

### OBJECTIVES

1. Select appropriate SharePoint site templates p. 7

2. Customize the look of sites p. 14

3. Create and edit lists and libraries p. 17

4. Add pages to existing sites p. 20

5. Define user roles and permissions p. 31

6. Implement versioning options p. 33

7. Manage workflows p. 34

### Prepare Case

Production & Operations

## Building a Corporate Site Collection

Aidan Matthews, CTO at the Painted Paradise Golf Resort and Spa, has decided that using SharePoint Online will provide a number of benefits for all areas of the company and has asked you to create the overall SharePoint site collection for the company.

After you have set up the overall site collection, Barry Cheney, manager of the Red Bluff Golf Club, would like to work with you to fully develop the sites needed for the Red Bluff Golf Club and its upcoming Putts for Paws charity tournament event.

© Eric Gevaert/Fotolia

### REAL WORLD SUCCESS

"Using our SharePoint site to centrally store all of our team documents, contact information, and calendar events has made it easier to know that I always have access to the most current version of the information that matters to me. SharePoint has improved our team's overall performance and efficiency."

—Julie, alumnus and manager

### Student data files needed for this workshop:

 sp01ws01ResortLogo.jpg

 sp01ws01GolfLogo.jpg

sp01ws01SpaLogo.jpg

sp01ws01LoungeLogo.jpg

sp01ws01Indigo5Logo.jpg

sp01ws01CoffeeLogo.jpg

 sp01ws01GiftsLogo.jpg

 sp01ws01EventsLogo.jpg

 sp01ws01RequestTemplate.xsn

### You will save your top-level site as:

sp01ws01PPR_LastFirst

### You will save your files as:

sp01ws01SiteMap_LastFirst.docx

sp01ws01Request_LastFirst.xml

# Creating a Site Collection

SharePoint Server is the Microsoft server software that provides the foundation for a collaborative workspace where users can have access to all of the information they need to effectively do their jobs in a central, online, and secure location.

A **site collection** within SharePoint Server consists of multiple related sites. In this next section, you will define the organizational hierarchy of a SharePoint site collection and create the sites in SharePoint using predefined templates.

## Access Your SharePoint Server

SharePoint Server 2013 can be installed on a Windows Server physically located within an organization's network infrastructure or is available through subscriptions to SharePoint Online or Office 365. Regardless of the physical location of the server machine, most users access specific SharePoint team sites through a web browser using login credentials provided by a server administrator.

### Signing In to SharePoint Server 2013

SharePoint Server is a permissions-based system that provides user-level access to one or more sites in the site collection based on an authenticated username and password. For internally hosted and managed SharePoint servers, most users will be provided a URL, or website address, for the organization's **top-level team site** as the starting point for a site collection providing a site homepage, a shared document library, and a notebook. When accessing the site, users may be prompted to provide a username and password.

For organizational subscriptions to SharePoint Online or Office 365, users will sign in using an organizational account through the Office 365 login page.

---

SIDE NOTE

**Account Required**

An account on an established SharePoint Server is required to complete the steps in this activity.

### sp01.00 To Access SharePoint Server 2013

a. Start your web browser, and then navigate to the SharePoint Server Team Site provided by your instructor.

b. If prompted, type your username and your password, and then click **Sign in**.

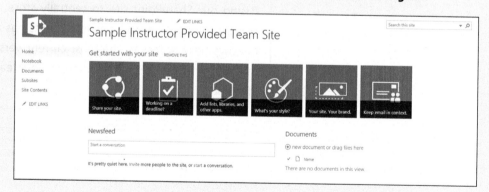

**Figure 1**   Sample instructor provided Team Site

c. If necessary, from the top menu, click **Sites**, and then click **Team Site** to access the top level team site and follow the navigation to the site specified by your instructor.

> **Troubleshooting**
> Screenshots are based on a default setup of a SharePoint Online account and may differ from customized installations of SharePoint Server in your environment.

## Visualize Site Hierarchy

Author Allen Lakein said "Failing to plan is planning to fail." Once SharePoint is implemented within an organization, users will become familiar with the site hierarchy and will access and contribute information in the site locations of greatest relevance to them. As such, it can be confusing to users if information is moved within the site hierarchy after initial development.

Proper planning and analysis of the business needs are key to determining the site hierarchy and deciding to implement a SharePoint site. As new sites are created, they are placed in the hierarchy relative to where they are created. When a new site is created, the active site is considered the **parent site**, and the new site is considered a **child site (subsite)** to the parent.

According to best practice, site structure is based on the information users in the organization need to access for collaboration and development. Each organization is different and has unique needs for the sharing of information. In many cases, the site hierarchy can be designed to follow a similar structure to the corporate hierarchy. In other cases, function-related sites and subsites may be more appropriate.

Consider the sample site hierarchy for Painted Paradise Resort and Spa shown in Figure 2. The top-level site for the resort is divided into nine subsites: seven representing the main areas of the resort based on the corporate structure, plus additional subsites for communication related to the SharePoint implementation process and a corporate-level blog. The Red Bluff Golf Course area is further divided into three subsites: one for the Red Bluff Pro Shop, one for the Red Bluff Bistro, and a third for the Red Bluff Putts for Paws charity tournament event. The Event Planning area is similarly divided into three subsites, one for each of the rooms available for hosting events at the resort.

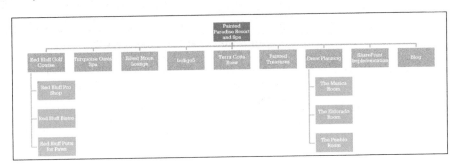

**Figure 2**   Sample site hierarchy for Painted Paradise Resort and Spa

In most cases, you will be provided access to a higher-level site as a member and be given permission to contribute to the libraries, lists, and collaborative elements in place on the site or a subsite. You may also be given additional rights to create sites of your own as you will have in this workshop.

### Using SmartArt Graphics in Word to Illustrate Hierarchy

Although many tools exist, such as Microsoft Visio, to generate organizational charts, the SmartArt feature of Microsoft Word is a sufficient tool for organizing ideas in a hierarchal form quickly and easily.

You will now open the Microsoft Word desktop application on your computer and build a SmartArt graphic to represent the Painted Paradise Resort and Spa SharePoint site hierarchy.

## sp01.01 To Create a SmartArt Graphic in Word

a. Open a new Blank Document in the Microsoft Word desktop application on your computer.

b. On the Quick Access Toolbar in Word, click **Save** 🔲, and then navigate to your desired storage location.

c. In the File Name box, type sp01ws01SiteMap_LastFirst, using your last and first name, and then click **Save**.

d. Click the **DESIGN** tab, and then in the Document Formatting group, click **Themes**, and then click **Damask**.

e. On the PAGE LAYOUT tab, in the Page Setup group, click **Orientation**, and then click **Landscape**.

f. On the INSERT tab, in the Illustrations group, click **SmartArt**.

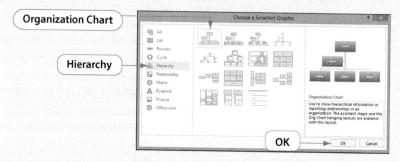

**Figure 3**    Choose a SmartArt Graphic dialog box

g. In the Choose a SmartArt Graphic dialog box, click the **Hierarchy** heading, click **Organization Chart**, and then click **OK**.

h. Click the outside border of the SmartArt graphic. On the SMARTART TOOLS DESIGN tab, in the SmartArt Styles group, click **Change Colors**, and then click **Colorful Range - Accent Colors 5 to 6**.

i. On the SMARTART TOOLS FORMAT tab, in the Size group, click **Width**, type 9" and then press Enter.

j. Click the top text placeholder, and then type Painted Paradise Resort and Spa.

k. Click the second text placeholder twice, and then press Del.

l. Click the first text placeholder on the second row, and then type Red Bluff Golf Course.

m. Click the second text placeholder on the second row, and then type Turquoise Oasis Spa.

n. Click the third text placeholder on the second row, and then type Silver Moon Lounge.

o. On the SMARTART TOOLS DESIGN tab, in the Create Graphic group, click the **Add Shape arrow**, and then click **Add Shape After**. Type Indigo5. Repeat this step five times for Terra Cotta Brew, Painted Treasures, Event Planning, SharePoint Implementation, and Blog.

p. Click the Red Bluff Golf Course placeholder. On the SMARTART TOOLS DESIGN tab, in the Create Graphic group, click the **Add Shape** button, and then type Red Bluff Pro Shop. Repeat this step twice for Red Bluff Bistro and Red Bluff Putts for Paws.

q. Click the Event Planning placeholder. On the SMARTART TOOLS DESIGN tab, in the Create Graphic group, click the **Add Shape** button, and then type The Musica Room. Repeat this step twice for The Eldorado Room and The Pueblo Room.

r.   Verify that the SmartArt graphic matches Figure 2, and then on the Quick Access Toolbar, click **Save** ⊟.

s.   Close Microsoft Word.

**REAL WORLD ADVICE**   Planning Permissions

When planning your site hierarchy, it may be useful to think about which team members will require access to which subsites. When possible, inheriting permissions from the parent site makes setup faster for individual team sites.

## Select Appropriate Site Templates

Each site on a SharePoint Server is based on a preconfigured **site template** that includes common lists and libraries related to the intended purpose of that site. Although site templates provide a foundation for quickly creating content and deploying the site, each business has unique needs for site settings, site elements, and other necessary changes that are applied after initial creation of the site in the collection.

The top-level team site in SharePoint is based on the **team site template** that contains basic components needed to immediately begin sharing documents, maintain a central team notebook, and create or organize information important to the team. The team site template is flexible enough to be used for most sites in the site collection.

A **blog template** allows for posting ideas with inherent commenting tools for site visitor use. Blogs can be used for communication of ideas at the corporate level or within specific areas of the site collection as desired. The commenting tools associated with the template make it easy for visitors to share their response to the postings and continue the discussion.

A **project site template** brings all status, communication, and artifacts relevant to a project into one place. Project sites make it easy for members of a team to keep up with the overall status of a project, remaining tasks, and relevant resources in a central location accessible by everyone involved in the process.

A **community site template** is a discussion-driven site where content can be searched, sorted, and rated. Members gain reputation points by participating in the community, starting discussions, replying to and liking posts, and by specifying best replies.

**QUICK REFERENCE**   Template Selection Guide

The common types of templates and their usage are listed below:

- Team Site—A place to work together with a group of people.
- Blog—A site for a person or team to post ideas, observations, and expertise that site visitors can comment on.
- Project Site—A site for managing and collaborating on a project.
- Community Site—A place where community members discuss topics of common interest.
- Document Center—A site to centrally manage documents in your enterprise.
- Records Center—This template creates a site designed for records management.
- Business Intelligence Center—A site for presenting Business Intelligence content in SharePoint.
- Enterprise Search Center—A site focused on delivering an enterprise-wide search experience.
- Basic Search Center—A site focused on delivering a basic search experience.
- Visio Process Repository—A site for viewing, sharing, and storing Visio process diagrams.
- SAP Workflow Site—An SAP Workflow site that aggregates all user business tasks.

> **CONSIDER THIS** | **Benefits to Different Site Templates**
>
> What are the benefits to using different site templates? Is there a one-size-fits-all template available in SharePoint? Is there a potential disadvantage to starting from a template?

## Creating a Team Site for the Organization

Organizational team sites often serve as the top-level site in a site collection. The SharePoint Administrator for the organization would use the new site option from the main SharePoint Server Sites page to create or manage top-level team sites as needed for the organization.

Within the SharePoint Server hierarchy, new team sites that do not inherit permissions from the parent site and serve as the parent to additional subsites can serve the same purpose of isolating a site collection for a department, division, or geographic site within a larger organization.

You will use this method of creating a unique site collection for Painted Paradise Golf Resort and Spa within an existing SharePoint Server site collection.

**sp01.02** **To Create a New Team Site**

a. If necessary, start your web browser, and then navigate to the SharePoint Server Team Site provided by your instructor.

b. Click **Site Contents**, and then click **new subsite**.

**SIDE NOTE**

**Using a Touch Device**
When interacting with SharePoint Server, you can substitute tap gestures in place of mouse clicks throughout the instructions.

Site Contents on Quick Launch

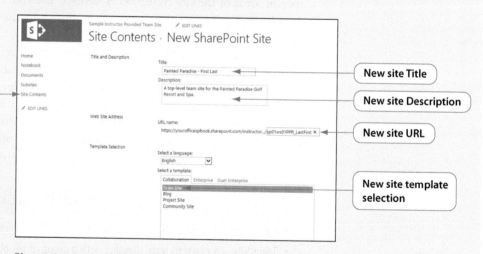

**Figure 4**    New SharePoint site window

c. In the **Title** box, type Painted Paradise – First Last, using your first and last name.

**d.** In the **Description** box, type A top-level team site for the Painted Paradise Golf Resort and Spa.

**e.** In the **URL name** box, delete any automatically generated text, and then type sp01ws01PPR_LastFirst, using your last and first name.

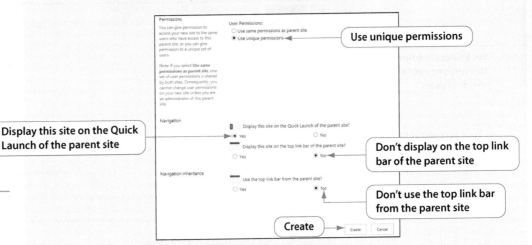

**Figure 5**    New site permissions and navigation

**f.** In the Permissions section, click **Use unique permissions**.

**g.** Under Display this site on the Quick Launch of the parent site?, click **Yes**.

**h.** Under Display this site on the top link bar of the parent site?, click **No**.

**i.** Click **Create**. Leave the People and Groups > Set Up Groups for this Site page open for the next activity.

## Assigning Groups to the New Site

SharePoint Server uses groups to separate users making it easier to manage permission settings throughout sites on multiple accounts at the same time. Groups must have unique names within the entire site collection and are often associated with the members' role on the site. Within SharePoint three basic **user roles** exist for each site: visitor, member, and owner.

**Visitors** to a site are typically granted read-only access to information contained in the site. This access allows the visitor to see the information without granting them permission to edit or delete content or site elements.

**Members** of a site are typically granted contribute permission, allowing them to contribute content to existing lists and libraries and edit page content, but they are not allowed to create additional lists and libraries or modify site structure or permissions.

**Owners** of a site are typically granted full control permission, which allows them to create, edit, add, and delete content, lists, libraries, site structure, and permissions.

By adding users in your organization to one or more of these site-level groups, you grant them the related permission level on the site. As the site creator, your account is automatically added to the member and owner groups.

You will now finish the setup of your top-level team site by creating a Visitor, a Member, and an Owner group and assign appropriate membership to each.

SIDE NOTE

**Using Unique Permissions**

Using unique permissions ensures that other users who have administrative rights to the parent site cannot view or edit your site content.

SIDE NOTE

**Navigation Settings**

Adding too many sites to the top link bar of the parent site can cause unnecessary horizontal scrolling.

## sp01.03 To Select and Assign Group Permissions

a. On the People and Groups > Set Up Groups for this Site page from the end of the previous activity, verify that group names have been automatically assigned to the new groups.

**Set Visitors membership to Everyone except external users**

**Your account should be listed in Members and Owners**

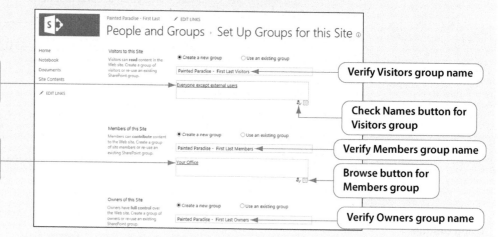

**Verify Visitors group name**

**Check Names button for Visitors group**

**Verify Members group name**

**Browse button for Members group**

**Verify Owners group name**

**Figure 6**    Set Up Groups for this Site

---

**Troubleshooting**

If group names are not automatically assigned, the site does not have a unique name or has been created and deleted. If you created the site previously and had cause to delete and recreate it, select Use an existing group, click More, locate the Painted Paradise – First Last Visitors, Painted Paradise – First Last Members, and Painted Paradise – First Last Owners groups previously created, and then click OK.

   If you have not created the site previously, type Painted Paradise 2 – First Last Visitors, type Painted Paradise 2 – First Last Members, and type Painted Paradise 2 – First Last Owners, using your first and last name, and replacing 2 with 3, 4, and so on until a unique group name is created, allowing you to continue.

---

**SIDE NOTE**

**Everyone User**

The Everyone user account refers to all SharePoint user accounts set up on the server.

**SIDE NOTE**

**Adding Users Directly**

If you know the user names for additional members to be added to specific groups, you can type them directly in the Group Members box separated by semicolons.

b. In the Visitors to this Site section, click the **Group Members** box, type Everyone and then click **Check Names** 🔍.

c. If a message is displayed stating "No exact match was found," click **Everyone**, click **Everyone except external users [All Users (per Tenant)]**, and then click **Check Names** 🔍.

d. In the Owners of this Site section, click **Browse** 📖.

e. In the **Find** box, type your instructor's last name and then press Enter.

f. Click to select your instructor from the list, click **Add ->**, and then click **OK**.

g. Verify that both you and your instructor are listed in the Owners of this Site **Group Members** box, and then click **OK**.

### Identifying Key Features of a Team Site

A newly created team site contains common features that make it easy to begin creating and sharing content with team members. As shown in Figure 7, each site and page within the site collection will follow a consistent layout and structure for common components including the top menu, Ribbon, top link bar, and Quick Launch.

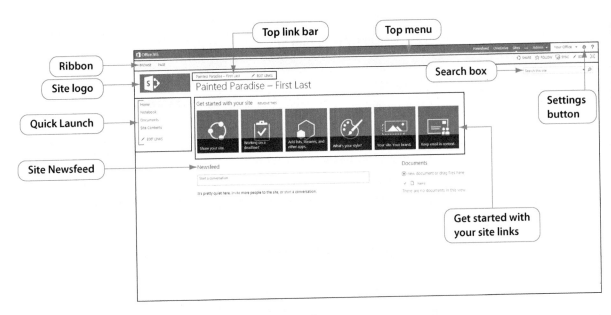

Top link bar

Top menu

Ribbon

Site logo

Quick Launch

Site Newsfeed

Search box

Settings button

Get started with your site links

**Figure 7**   Painted Paradise Team Site

At the very top of the page, the **top menu** in SharePoint provides access to various features of SharePoint, profile options, settings, and help features.

Below the top menu, the **Ribbon** is the tabbed interface containing the BROWSE tab, core page control buttons, and other context-sensitive buttons and tabs depending on the page being viewed. Core controls available for pages in SharePoint are SHARE, FOLLOW, SYNC, and EDIT or SAVE buttons located on the right edge of the Ribbon.

The **top link bar** appears below the Ribbon and provides navigation to the homepage of the current site and includes a search bar. It can be configured to include links to any subsites that may exist from that site or to inherit links from the parent site.

The **Quick Launch**, or left side menu area, in a SharePoint site provides access to all of the other content areas created by or available to the site template.

## Create Additional Sites and Subsites

Once the top-level site has been created for a site collection, or a portion of the defined site hierarchy, the same process can be used with appropriate selections to create the remaining sites in the collection. As additional sites and subsites are added to the collection, it is important to navigate to the appropriate parent site before creating the new subsite.

Additional consideration should be given for the placement of a link to the new subsite on the Quick Launch or top link bar of the parent site as well as the permissions needed for the subsite in relation to the groups already existing at the parent site.

### Creating Team Sites for Organizational Teams

Once you have planned your site hierarchy and have established the top-level team site on the SharePoint Server, additional subsites can be created to complete the site collection. You will now use the site hierarchy created earlier to build additional team sites for the various businesses that operate within the Painted Paradise Golf Resort and Spa.

**sp01.04 To Create a Team Subsite**

a. If necessary, start your web browser, and then navigate to your Painted Paradise – First Last site.

b. Click **Site Contents**, and then click **new subsite**.

c. In the **Title** box, type Red Bluff Golf Course.

d. In the **URL name** box, type RBGC.

e. Under Display this site on the Quick Launch of the parent site?, click **Yes**, and then under Display this site on the top link bar of the parent site?, click **No**.

f. Under Use the top link bar from the parent site?, click **Yes**, and then click **Create**.

g. Click **Painted Paradise – First Last** on the top link bar.

h. Repeat the above steps for the other organizational teams using the following titles and URL names.

| Title | URL Name |
|---|---|
| Turquoise Oasis Spa | spa |
| Silver Moon Lounge | lounge |
| Indigo5 | indigo5 |
| Terra Cotta Brew | coffee |
| Painted Treasures | gifts |
| Event Planning | events |

i. If necessary, click **Painted Paradise – First Last** on the top link bar to return to the parent site, and then in the Quick Launch, click **Red Bluff Golf Course**.

j. Click **Site Contents**, and then click **new subsite**.

k. In the **Title** box, type Pro Shop, and then in the **URL name** box, type proshop.

l. Under Display this site on the Quick Launch of the parent site?, click **Yes**.

m. Under Use the top link bar from the parent site?, click **Yes**, and then click **Create**.

n. Repeat Steps i through m to create an additional subsite for the Red Bluff Bistro. In the **Title** box, type Bistro, and then in the **URL name** box, type bistro.

o. If necessary, click **Painted Paradise – First Last** on the top link bar to return to the parent site, and then in the Quick Launch, click **Event Planning**.

p. Create three subsites to the Event Planning site using the following titles and URL names and click **Yes** under the Display this site on the Quick Launch of the parent site? and under the Use the top link bar from the parent site? for each subsite.

| Title | URL Name |
|---|---|
| The Musica Room | musica |
| The Eldorado Room | eldorado |
| The Pueblo Room | pueblo |

### Creating Project Sites

Project sites bring all status, communication, and artifacts relevant to a project into one place. Project sites make it easy for members of a team to keep up with the overall status of a project, remaining tasks, and relevant resources in a central location accessible by everyone involved in the process.

The CTO, Aidan Matthews, has decided that it would be beneficial to all involved to create a project site for the overall implementation of SharePoint sites at Painted Paradise Golf Resort and Spa.

You will now add a project site to the site hierarchy as a subsite to the top-level team site.

### sp01.05 To Create a Project Subsite

a. If necessary, start your web browser, and then navigate to your Painted Paradise – First Last site.

b. Click **Site Contents**, and then click **new subsite**.

c. In the **Title** box, type SharePoint Implementation.

d. In the **URL name** box, type SharePoint.

e. Under the Template Selection section, on the Collaboration tab, click **Project Site**.

f. Under Use the top link bar from the parent site?, click **Yes**, and then click **Create**.

### Creating a Community Site

Community sites are discussion-driven sites where content can be searched, sorted, and rated. Members gain reputation points by participating in the community, starting discussions, replying to and liking posts, and by specifying best replies.

Barry Cheney, manager of the Red Bluff Golf Club, has decided that this site template would best meet the needs for sharing information about the upcoming Red Bluff Putts for Paws charity event. You will now add a community subsite to the Red Bluff Golf Course for the Red Bluff Putts for Paws event.

### sp01.06 To Create a Community Subsite

a. If necessary, start your web browser, and then navigate to your Painted Paradise – First Last site.

b. In the Quick Launch, click **Red Bluff Golf Course**.

c. Click **Site Contents**, and then click **new subsite**.

d. In the **Title** box, type Red Bluff Putts for Paws.

e. In the **URL name** box, type charity.

f. Under the Template Selection section, on the Collaboration tab, click **Community Site**.

g. Under Display this site on the Quick Launch of the parent site?, click **Yes**.

h. Under Use the top link bar from the parent site?, click **Yes**.

i. Click **Create**.

### Creating a Blog

Blog sites allow for posting ideas with inherent commenting tools for site visitor use. Blogs can be used for communication of ideas at the corporate level or within specific areas of the site collection as desired. The commenting tools associated with the template make it easy for visitors to share their response to the postings and continue the discussion.

The CEO, William Mattingly, has decided that a corporate blog on SharePoint will improve communication with all employees and provide a place for discussion and feedback.

You will now create the blog site for Painted Paradise Golf Resort and Spa.

### sp01.07 To Create a Blog Site

a. If necessary, start your web browser, and then navigate to your Painted Paradise – First Last site.

b. Click **Site Contents**, and then click **new subsite**.

c. In the **Title** box, type Blog.

d. In the **URL name** box, type blog.

e. Under the Template Selection section, on the Collaboration tab, click **Blog**.

f. Under Use the top link bar from the parent site?, click **Yes**.

g. Click **Create**.

## Customizing Site Contents

Each site template provides core apps, lists, and libraries specific to the selected site type that are ready for users to create and edit site content. Simply using these pre-configured features may be sufficient for the intended purpose of the site; however, in most cases, site owners will want to personalize the site through the application of themes, incorporation of corporate logos, or addition of custom apps, lists, libraries, and pages to meet the unique needs of the site.

In this next section you will personalize the sites that you have created, install apps, lists, and libraries, and add content to the sites.

### Change the Look of the Site

The visual appearance of a site collection or individual sites can be adjusted through the application of themes and modification of the logo displayed on the site.

A **theme** provides a consistent look and feel to your SharePoint site by consistently applying fonts and colors throughout the site and is important to a business's branding. A selection of theme choices are installed by default in SharePoint Server and additional themes may be uploaded for use to meet specific business standards in place at a company. Applying a theme does not affect the positioning of web parts on the site pages.

A **logo** is an image file placed in the upper left corner of the site pages to the left of the top link bar and above the Quick Launch. Applying a logo to a site adds a corporate identity to the site pages and content.

### Adding a Logo to Your Site

To better brand Painted Paradise on the site, you will now replace the default logos on the created sites with custom logos for the divisions of the Painted Paradise Golf Resort and Spa.

## sp01.08 To Add a Logo to a Team Site

a. If necessary, start your web browser, and then navigate to your Painted Paradise – First Last site.

b. Click **Settings** ⚙, and then click **Site settings**.

c. Under the Look and Feel heading, click **Title, description, and logo**.

d. Under Insert Logo, click **FROM COMPUTER**.

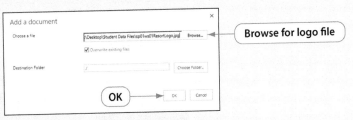

Figure 8 Add a document dialog box

e. In the Add a document dialog box, click **Browse**, locate and select the **sp01ws01Resort-Logo** file in your student data files, click **Open**, and then click **OK**.

f. Click **OK**, and then in the top link bar, click **Painted Paradise – First Last**.

g. Repeat the above steps, adding the appropriate logos from your student data files to each of the subsites that have been created, as follows.

| Subsite | Logo File |
|---|---|
| Red Bluff Golf Course | sp01ws01GolfLogo |
| Turquoise Oasis Spa | sp01ws01SpaLogo |
| Silver Moon Lounge | sp01ws01LoungeLogo |
| Indigo5 | sp01ws01Indigo5Logo |
| Terra Cotta Brew | sp01ws01CoffeeLogo |
| Painted Treasures | sp01ws01GiftsLogo |
| Event Planning | sp01ws01EventsLogo |
| Pro Shop | sp01ws01GolfLogo |
| Bistro | sp01ws01GolfLogo |
| The Musica Room | sp01ws01EventsLogo |
| The Eldorado Room | sp01ws01EventsLogo |
| The Pueblo Room | sp01ws01EventsLogo |
| SharePoint Implementation | sp01ws01ResortLogo |
| Red Bluff Putts for Paws | sp01ws01GolfLogo |
| Blog | sp01ws01ResortLogo |

### Applying a Site Theme

In addition to logo usage, themes can aid in the application of colors, fonts, layouts, and general image throughout major sections of your site collection, representing individual areas with visual consistency. You will now apply themes to the main resort site and the Red Bluff Golf Course site and subsites.

**sp01.09 To Change the Site Theme**

a. If necessary, start your web browser, and then navigate to your Painted Paradise – First Last site.

b. Click **Settings** ⚙, and then click **Change the look**.

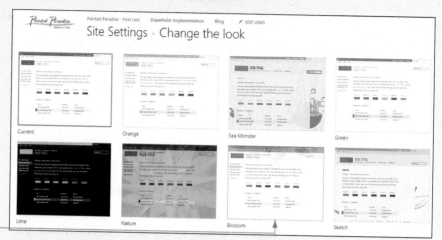

Blossom theme

**Figure 9** Change the look

c. Click **Blossom**, then click **Try it out**, and then click **Yes, keep it**.

d. Repeat Steps b and c for the SharePoint Implementation and Blog subsites.

e. Navigate to your Red Bluff Golf Course subsite, click **Settings** ⚙, and then click **Change the look**.

f. Click **Breeze**.

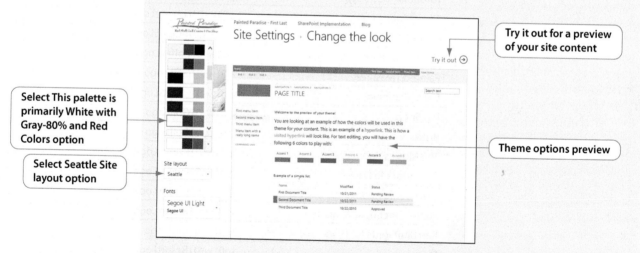

Select This palette is primarily White with Gray-80% and Red Colors option

Select Seattle Site layout option

Try it out for a preview of your site content

Theme options preview

**Figure 10** Theme options

g. Click **Colors**, and then click **This palette is primarily White with Gray-80% and Red**.

h. Click **Try it out**, and then click **Yes, keep it**.

i. Repeat Steps e through h for the Pro Shop, Bistro, and Red Bluff Putts for Paws subsites.

## Add Lists, Libraries, and Other Apps

SharePoint apps are used to extend the functionality of sites. An **App** in SharePoint refers to a list, library, or other configurable component for creating or maintaining site content.

A **list** is used to store and manage information, such as tasks or calendar events, organized into columns of information representing specific attributes of each item in the list. A **view** is applied to lists to show specific columns, filter the results shown, and apply sorts to the values entered.

A **library** is a special purpose list that is used to store files and information about those files. A library contains columns representing the information related to each file including the name of the file, the dates when the file was created and last modified, and who created or modified the file.

SharePoint includes five types of libraries: document libraries, form libraries, picture libraries, slide libraries, and Wiki page libraries. Each has a specific purpose.

**Document libraries** provide a place for storing documents or other files that you want to share. Document libraries allow folders, versioning, and check out.

**Form libraries** are a place to manage business forms like status reports or purchase orders. Form libraries require a compatible XML editor, such as Microsoft InfoPath.

**Picture libraries** are a place to upload and share pictures.

**Slide libraries** allow for the sharing of slides from Microsoft PowerPoint, or a compatible application, and provide special features for finding, managing, and reusing slides.

**Wiki page libraries** are an interconnected set of easily editable web pages, which can contain text, images, and web parts. Wiki page libraries are the basis for editable pages, like the homepage, in the team site template.

### Adding a Form Library to Your Site

A form library is a place to manage business forms like status reports or purchase orders. Form libraries require a compatible XML editor, such as Microsoft InfoPath. Using a form library ensures consistency of data entry and minimizes storage requirements on the SharePoint Server by storing only the entered data rather than the form structure for each new form in the library.

You will now add a form library to the SharePoint Implementation site for users to be able to request the creation of additional sites within the site collection or improvements to existing sites.

### sp01.10 To Add a Form Library

a. If necessary, start your web browser, and then navigate to your SharePoint Implementation subsite.

b. Click **Site Contents**, and then click **add an app**.

c. Under the Apps you can add heading, click **Form Library**.

**Figure 11** Add an App

d. In the **Name** box, type Implementation Requests and then click **Create**.

### Adding a Discussion Board

A **discussion board** provides a threaded message board that is available to all members of the team without cluttering the team members' inbox with unnecessary e-mail messages. By using the discussion board on the team site instead of e-mail, the entire conversation related to a thread is kept together. Alerts can be set on individual threads to be sure that new contributions to important conversations are not overlooked.

You will now create a discussion board on the main resort site for the exchange of ideas among all resort employees.

### sp01.11 **To Add a Discussion Board**

a. If necessary, start your web browser, and then navigate to your Painted Paradise – First Last site.

b. Click **Site Contents**, and then click **add an app**.

c. Under the Apps you can add heading, click **Discussion Board**.

d. In the **Name** box, type Idea Exchange and then click **Create**.

### Adding a Calendar App

A **calendar app** provides a central location for listing events and activities that impact the team as a whole or resources shared by team members. The calendar app provides the ability to share team members' schedules and to view scheduled events for a specific day, week, or month at a glance. As a web part on site pages, the view also includes summary options for current events that link to the full details in the calendar list.

You will now add a calendar app to the Pro Shop subsite to keep track of appointments.

### sp01.12 To Add a Calendar App

a. If necessary, start your web browser, and then navigate to your Pro Shop subsite.

b. Click **Site Contents**, and then click **add an app**.

c. Under the Apps you can add heading, click **Calendar**.

d. In the Adding Calendar dialog box, click **Advanced Options**.

e. In the **Name** box, type Pro Shop Calendar.

f. Under Use this calendar to share member's schedule?, click **Yes**, and then click **Create**.

### Adding a Custom List

**Custom lists** can be created for any information that can be consistently represented by predetermined fields. Each list template in SharePoint can be customized to add, rename, or delete fields from a default set associated with the list, but a custom list provides no initial structure and can be defined for the specific purpose within the site.

You will now create a custom list to keep track of corporate sponsors associated with the Red Bluff Putts for Paws charity golf tournament.

### sp01.13 To Create a Custom List

a. If necessary, start your web browser, and then navigate to your Red Bluff Putts for Paws subsite.

b. Click **Site Contents**, and then click **add an app**.

c. Under the Noteworthy heading, click **Custom List**.

d. In the **Name** box, type Corporate Sponsors and then click **Create**.

e. On the Quick Launch, click **Corporate Sponsors**.

f. On the LIST tab, in the Settings group, click **List Settings**.

g. Under the Columns heading, click **Title**.

h. If necessary, select the word Title in the **Column name** box, press ⌈Del⌉, and then type Company Name.

i. Under Enforce unique values, click **Yes**, and then click **OK**.

> **Troubleshooting**
> If a Message from webpage dialog box appears indicating that this column must be indexed to enforce unique values, click OK.

j. Under the Columns heading, click **Create column**.

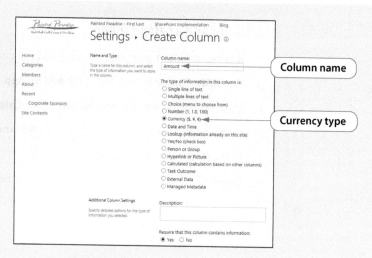

**Figure 12** Create Column

k. In the **Column name** box, type Amount and then click **Currency ($, ¥, €)**.

l. Under Require that this column contains information, click **Yes**, and then click **OK**.

m. On the Quick Launch, click **Corporate Sponsors**. The added column will display under the Columns heading.

---

**QUICK REFERENCE** | **Built-in Apps You Can Add**

**Libraries:** Document Library, Form Library, Wiki Page Library, Picture Library, Data Connection Library, Asset Library, Report Library
**Basic Lists:** Links, Promoted Links, Tasks, Custom List, Custom List in Datasheet View, External List
**Other Apps:** Announcements, Contacts, Calendar, Discussion Board, Issue Tracking, Survey, Access App, Import Spreadsheet, Site Mailbox

---

**REAL WORLD ADVICE** | **More Apps at the SharePoint Store**

If the built-in apps do not meet your needs, a wide array of free and paid apps can be quickly downloaded and installed from the SharePoint store. From the add an app area in SharePoint, you can directly access the SharePoint store from the Quick Launch to purchase and/or install apps from a variety of categories to meet specific needs.

---

## Add More Pages to Your Site

Within sites, additional pages can help organize content into manageable and identifiable sections of information. Each page is represented within the Wiki page library for the site, has a unique address, and is given an appropriate name at the time of creation. App Parts and Web Parts can be added to the pages to represent content in other apps, lists, or libraries, or text, images, and other media content generated specifically for the selected page.

In this section, you will explore the Wiki page library, create new pages in the library, and add links to the new pages on the Quick Launch for the Red Bluff Golf Course Pro Shop site.

### Exploring the Wiki Page Library

Each SharePoint site is a collection of pages managed by a Wiki page library. A Wiki page library is an interconnected set of easily editable web pages, which can contain text, images, and web parts. Wiki page libraries are the basis for editable pages, like the homepage, in the team site template.

You will now explore the Wiki page library for the Red Bluff Golf Course Pro Shop subsite.

### sp01.14 To Access the Site Pages

a. If necessary, start your web browser, and then navigate to your Red Bluff Golf Course Pro Shop subsite.

b. On the PAGE tab, in the Page Library group, click **View All Pages**.

**How To Use This Library page link**

**New Wiki page**

**Figure 13** Wiki Page library

c. Click **How To Use This Library**.

d. In the Quick Launch, click **Home**.

### Creating a New Wiki Page

Mr. Cheney has decided that it would be helpful to create two additional pages on the Red Bluff Golf Course Pro Shop subsite: one to list current specials, and the other to post golf pro tips.

You will now create two new Wiki pages in the Red Bluff Golf Course Pro Shop Wiki page library.

### sp01.15 To Create a New Wiki Page

a. If necessary, start your web browser, and then navigate to your Red Bluff Golf Course Pro Shop subsite.

b. On the PAGE tab, in the Page Library group, click **View All Pages**.

c. Click **new Wiki page**.

d. In the **New page name** box, type Current Specials and then click **Create**.

e. On the FORMAT TEXT tab, in the Styles group, click **Heading 1**.

f. Type Current Specials and press Enter.

g. On the FORMAT TEXT tab, in the Edit group, click **Save**.

h. On the PAGE tab, in the Page Library group, click **View All Pages**.

i. Click **new Wiki page**.

j. In the **New page name** box, type Golf Pro Tips and then click **Create**.

k. On the FORMAT TEXT tab, in the Styles group, click **Heading 1**.

l. Type Golf Pro Tips and press Enter.

m. On the FORMAT TEXT tab, in the Edit group, click **Save**.

n. In the Quick Launch, click **Home**.

---

**REAL WORLD ADVICE** | Using a Different Page as the Site Homepage

If you want to use a different page from the Wiki page library as the homepage for a site, you can designate a new homepage by navigating to the new page and on the PAGE tab, in the Page Actions group, click Make Homepage, and then click OK.

---

### Adding a Page to the Quick Launch

To make the pages more accessible to the end user, it is helpful to add a link to the page to the Quick Launch or top link bar of the SharePoint site. You will now add links to the Current Specials and Golf Pro Tips pages on the Quick Launch of the Red Bluff Golf Course Pro Shop site.

---

**sp01.16 To Add a Page Link to the Quick Launch**

a. If necessary, start your web browser, and then navigate to your Red Bluff Golf Course Pro Shop subsite.

b. On the PAGE tab, in the Page Library group, click **View All Pages**.

c. In the Quick Launch, click **EDIT LINKS**.

d. In the Site Pages list, right-click Current Specials, and then click **Copy shortcut**.

e. In the Quick Launch, click **link**.

**Figure 14**   Add a Link dialog box

f. In **Text to display**, type Current Specials, press Tab, then press Ctrl+V, and then click **OK**.

g. In the Site Pages list, right-click Golf Pro Tips, and then click **Copy shortcut**.

h.  In the Quick Launch, click **link**.

i.  In **Text to display**, type Golf Pro Tips, press ⎡Tab⎤, then press ⎡Ctrl⎤+⎡V⎤, and then click **OK**.

j.  In the Quick Launch, drag **Current Specials** below Home, drag **Golf Pro Tips** below Current Specials, and then click **Save**.

k.  In the Quick Launch, click **Home**.

---

**CONSIDER THIS** | **SharePoint Site Similarities/Differences Compared to Other Websites**

In what ways is the display of content and navigation in SharePoint sites similar to that of other commercial websites you have experienced? In what ways are they different?

## Edit Page Contents

One of the first places to begin personalizing a team site is on the homepage. By editing the homepage, you can provide a clear identity to the site and adjust web parts to be certain that the most relevant information is displayed first to users and visitors of the site.

### Editing the Homepage

The homepage of a site is a common place to provide a greeting or important information for all visitors to easily find. Mr. Cheney wants to be sure that the upcoming charity tournament is clearly linked from the homepage and has drafted a welcome message to use on the Red Bluff Golf Course team site.

You will now edit the homepage of the Red Bluff Golf Course team site to include Mr. Cheney's welcome message and a link to the Red Bluff Putts for Paws golf tournament page in the site.

### sp01.17 To Edit Homepage Content

a.  Navigate to the homepage of the Red Bluff Golf Course.

b.  Above the Get started with your site tiles, click **REMOVE THIS**. If prompted to confirm removal, click **OK**.

c.  On the Ribbon, click the **Edit** button.

d.  At the top of the page, click in the empty placeholder. On the FORMAT TEXT tab, in the Styles group, click **Heading 1**. Type Welcome to Red Bluff Golf Course and then press ⎡Enter⎤.

e.  Type Thank you for visiting our team site. Check out the Newsfeed below and visit all that we have to offer on the course. Be sure to check out our Pro Shop and Bistro sites from the main menu to the left. Press ⎡Enter⎤. Type For more information on the upcoming Red Bluff Putts for Paws golf tournament, click here.

f.  Select the text **click here** at the end of the last paragraph.

g.  On the INSERT tab, in the Links group, click **Link**, and then click **From SharePoint**.

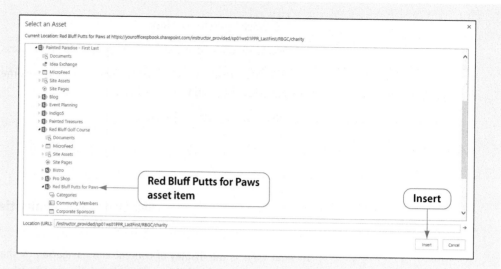

**Figure 15** Select an Asset

h. Click the **Red Bluff Putts for Paws** item, and then click **Insert**.

i. On the PAGE tab, in the Edit group, click **Save**.

## Adding an App Part to the Homepage

The Pro Shop Calendar app, added earlier to the Pro Shop subsite, provides team members a clear view of upcoming appointments by team member; however, team members have asked to have easier access to this information. By adding an App Part to the homepage, key information can be available to team members without additional navigation steps. You will now add the Pro Shop Calendar app to the Pro Shop homepage as an App Part.

### sp01.18 To Add an App Part to the Homepage

a. Navigate to the Pro Shop subsite, and then above the Get started with your site tiles, click **REMOVE THIS**. If prompted to confirm removal, click **OK.**

b. On the Ribbon, click the **Edit** button.

c. At the top of the page, click in the empty placeholder.

d. On the INSERT tab, in the Parts group, click **App Part.**

**Figure 16** Insert App Part

e. Under the Parts heading, click **Pro Shop Calendar**, and then click **Add**.

f. On the PAGE tab, in the Edit group, click **Save**.

Editing the view on Web Parts added to site pages can ensure that users are presented with the most relevant information for their needs. Using views with only key information on Web Parts added to the homepage can also save space while providing a link to the full list, library, or app if additional details are needed.

### Editing Other Site Pages

Mr. Cheney has decided that he wants a page added to the charity event subsite to promote corporate sponsors of the upcoming tournament. You will now create an additional page on the Red Bluff Putts for Paws subsite for corporate sponsors and add the Corporate Sponsors custom list app to the new page.

### sp01.19 To Add Content to an Additional Site Page

a. Navigate to the Red Bluff Putts for Paws subsite.

b. On the PAGE tab, in the Page Library group, click **View All Pages**.

c. Click **new Wiki page**.

d. In the **New page name** box, type Corporate Sponsors and then click **Create**.

e. On the FORMAT TEXT tab, in the Styles group, click **Heading 1**.

f. Type Corporate Sponsors and then press Enter.

g. Type We would like to thank the following sponsors for their generous contributions to our Red Bluff Putts for Paws tournament. Press Enter.

h. On the INSERT tab, in the Parts group, click **App Part**.

i. Under the Parts heading, click **Corporate Sponsors**, and then click **Add**.

j. On the PAGE tab, in the Edit group, click **Save**.

## Add Contents to Lists and Libraries

As a tool for business-critical information storage and collaboration, the success of a team site relies on the active contribution, review, and use of information in the libraries and lists contained on the site. Users listed in the site's Members group are given access permissions to create content within any lists, libraries, and page content areas that have not been restricted by advanced permission settings.

### Modifying the Form Library Template

**Microsoft InfoPath** provides the technology for designing form templates that can be published to SharePoint Form Libraries as well as the technology for filling out forms associated with the libraries in place on a SharePoint site. **Form templates** are applied to form libraries to consistently collect the data stored in the library.

Compared to a document library, the storage requirements for a form library are minimal given that only the form data, and not the document structure, is saved for each instance of the form. The InfoPath Services feature of SharePoint Server can be disabled by the SharePoint administrator for an organization and must be enabled to publish form templates to the form libraries.

You will now add a custom form template to the Implementation Requests form library on the SharePoint Implementation site.

SIDE NOTE

**Library Templates**

Using document or form templates with libraries in SharePoint ensures consistency of format across the files stored in the library.

a. Navigate to the SharePoint Implementation site, and then click **Implementation Requests** in the Quick Launch.

> **Troubleshooting**
>
> If Implementation Requests is not listed on the Quick Launch, click Site Contents, and then click Implementation Requests. If the app has not been created, complete the earlier activity sp01.10 before continuing.

b. Using File Explorer, navigate to your Student Data Files folder, and right-click on **sp01ws01RequestTemplate.xsn**, and then click **Copy**.

c. Return to the Implementation Requests page in your web browser. On the LIBRARY tab, in the Connect & Export group, click **Open with Explorer**.

> **Troubleshooting**
>
> If an Internet Explorer Security warning appears, click Allow to continue and repeat Step c.

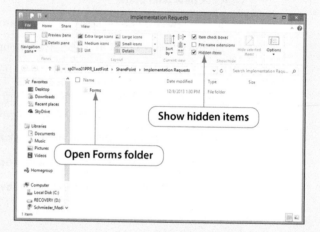

**Figure 17**   Implementation Requests Explorer window

d. In the Implementation Requests Explorer window, double-click the **Forms** folder, right-click in a blank area in the folder window, and then click **Paste**.

> **Troubleshooting**
>
> If the Forms folder is not visible in the Implementation Requests Explorer window, on the View tab, in the Show/hide group, check the Hidden items box.

e. Close File Explorer and return to the Implementation Requests page in your web browser.

f. On the LIBRARY tab, in the Settings group, click **Library Settings**.

g. Under the General Settings heading, click **Advanced settings**.

h. Select the text in the **Template URL** box, and then press Del.

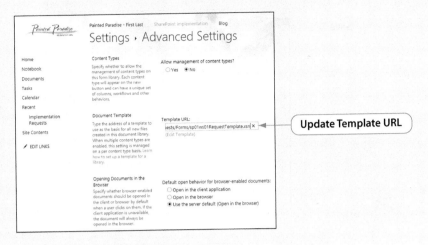

**Figure 18** Advanced Settings

i. Type Implementation Requests/Forms/sp01ws01RequestTemplate.xsn and then click **OK**.

j. On the Quick Launch, click **Implementation Requests**.

### Creating a New Document in a Form Library

Once a form template has been applied to a form library, users who create new items in the library are presented with a form matching the template structure, and they simply fill in the required fields inside their web browser and save the new document. Using the form template, you will now add a new item to the Implementation Requests form library.

### sp01.21 To Create a New Document in the Form Library

a. If necessary, navigate to the SharePoint Implementation site, and then click **Implementation Requests** on the Quick Launch.

b. On the FILES tab, in the New group, click **New Document**, and then click **OK**.

> **Troubleshooting**
> This process requires Microsoft Internet Explorer 7.0 or later and a Microsoft SharePoint Foundation-compatible XML editor such as Microsoft InfoPath. If prompted to allow this website to open a program on your computer, click Allow and provide e-mail address and password if prompted.

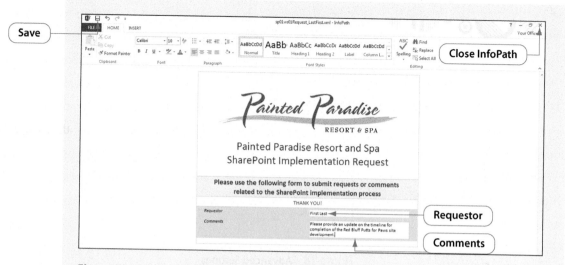

**Figure 19** New Implementation Request form

c. In the **Requestor** box, type your first and last name.

d. In the **Comments** box, type Please provide an update on the timeline for completion of the Red Bluff Putts for Paws site development.

e. If the form opened in your browser, on the EDIT tab, in the Commit group, click **Save**. If open in the InfoPath desktop application, on the Quick Access Toolbar, click **Save**.

f. In the **File name** box, type sp01ws01Request_LastFirst and then click **Save**.

g. If the form opened in your browser, on the EDIT tab, in the Commit group, click **Close**. If open in the InfoPath desktop application, close the open application.

## Posting to a Discussion Board

A community site template, as used by the Red Bluff Putts for Paws subsite, is centered on discussion among site members. In a community site, content can be searched, sorted, and rated. Members gain reputation points by participating in the community, starting discussions, replying to and liking posts, and specifying best replies.

You will now create an initial post to the community discussion board.

### sp01.22 To Add a New Discussion to the Discussion Board

a. Navigate to the Red Bluff Putts for Paws subsite.

b. Click **new discussion**.

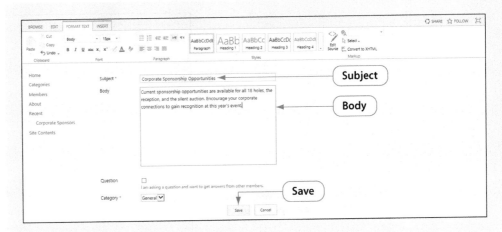

**Figure 20** New discussion

c. In the **Subject** box, type Corporate Sponsorship Opportunities and press [Tab].

d. In the **Body** box, type Current sponsorship opportunities are available for all 18 holes, the reception, and the silent auction. Encourage your corporate connections to gain recognition at this year's event.

e. Click **Save**.

---

**REAL WORLD ADVICE**    **Effective Conversation Starters**

When creating initial posts to discussion forums, consider using subjects that will encourage users to read the entire post. Follow up an engaging subject with a thought-provoking message post that will encourage readers to continue the discussion.

---

### Creating a Calendar Event

The Pro Shop Calendar app on the Pro Shop site is intended to keep track of all scheduled events for team members at the Red Bluff Pro Shop. You will now create an event on the Pro Shop Calendar for putting practice next Monday at 10 A.M.

### sp01.23 To Add a New Event to the Calendar

a. Navigate to the Pro Shop subsite, and then click the **Pro Shop Calendar** link above the calendar App Part on the homepage.

b. On the EVENTS tab, in the New group, click **New Event**.

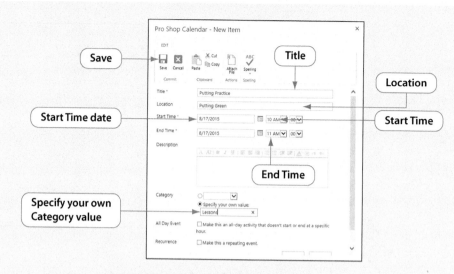

**Figure 21**    Pro Shop Calendar - New Item

c. In the **Title** box, type Putting Practice and then press [Tab].

d. In the **Location** box, type Putting Green and then press [Tab].

e. In the **Start Time** box, type next Monday's date and then select **10 AM**.

f. In the **End Time** box, verify that next Monday's date has been entered, and then select **11 AM**.

g. Under the Category heading, click the **Specify your own value** option, and then type Lessons.

h. Click **Save**.

**SIDE NOTE**

**Recurring Events**

Events that repeat on a regular schedule can easily be added with Daily, Weekly, Monthly, or Yearly patterns of recurrence when creating a new calendar item.

### Adding an Item to a Custom List

As additional information becomes available for lists within the site structure, users will contribute that content by adding new items to the existing lists. The Painted Paradise Golf Resort and Spa has made a contribution to the charity event as a corporate sponsor and the contribution needs to be recorded in the custom list created earlier.

You will now add the Painted Paradise Golf Resort and Spa as the first corporate sponsor on the Corporate Sponsors list on the Red Bluff Putts for Paws site.

### sp01.24 To Add an Item to a Custom List

a. Navigate to the Red Bluff Putts for Paws subsite, and click **Corporate Sponsors** in the Quick Launch.

b. Click **new item**.

c. In the **Company Name** box, type Painted Paradise Golf Resort and Spa and press [Tab].

d. In the **Amount** box, type 1000 and then click **Save**.

# Managing Permissions, Versioning, and Workflows

Advanced features of SharePoint include management tools for controlling access to site content through permissions, maintaining copies of files stored in document libraries for disaster recovery, and controlling the business processes through logical workflows attached to lists and libraries.

These options are typically managed by the site owner or a SharePoint administrator to ensure consistency with corporate standards and business rules.

## Define User Roles and Permissions

Content control within a SharePoint site is defined through user roles and permissions. **Permissions** define the level of access that is granted to a site, page, list, library, or item. In SharePoint, permissions can be set for people or groups.

**Groups** are created with unique names to represent multiple people, or individual users, within the organization. Naming groups based on a user's role or function within the organization or based on the way that a user interacts with the SharePoint site makes them easier to identify when applying permissions.

Users can be identified individually or as part of one or more groups. Establishing the correct permission level for each user and group in your organization is critical to maintaining a secure online environment for collaboration. Individual users can be added to existing groups to simplify permission management tasks.

### Editing Site Permissions

Site permissions are established when the site is created by either inheriting permission from the parent site or by creating new groups for site visitors, members, and owners. The default permissions associated with these roles are granted to individuals within the groups for accessing and editing site contents.

In the Painted Paradise Golf Resort and Spa site hierarchy, the Blog currently inherits permissions from the top-level team site and therefore grants contribute rights to all users in the Members group for that site. Mr. Mattingly has decided that only those individuals who are members of the Owners group should have rights to contribute to the blog site content and has asked that the Members group be limited to read-only access to the blog site content.

You will now edit the permissions on the Blog site to stop inheriting permissions from the parent site and limit the Members group access to Read-only permission levels.

### sp01.25 To Edit Site Permissions

**a.** Navigate to the Blog site, click the **Settings** button, and then click **Site settings**.

**b.** Under the Users and Permissions heading, click **Site permissions**.

**Stop Inheriting Permissions**

**Inheritance message**

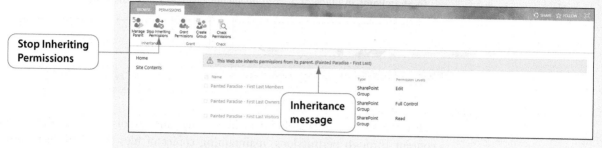

**Figure 22** Site permissions

**c.** On the PERMISSIONS tab, in the Inheritance group, click **Stop Inheriting Permissions**, and then click **OK**.

**d.** On the People and Groups > Set Up Groups for this Site page, click **OK**.

**e.** Click the **Settings** button, and then click **Site settings**.

**f.** Under the Users and Permissions heading, click **Site permissions**.

**g.** Click to select the check box next to **Painted Paradise – First Last Members**.

**h.** On the PERMISSIONS tab, in the Modify group, click **Edit User Permissions**.

**Clear the Edit check box**

**Uncheck Contribute**

**Select the Read check box**

**OK**

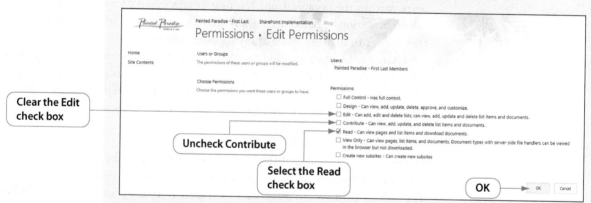

**Figure 23** Edit User Permissions

**i.** Click to uncheck **Edit** and **Contribute**, click to check **Read**, and then click **OK**.

**j.** Click **Home** in the Quick Launch.

---

**REAL WORLD ADVICE**  **Permission Management**

Whenever possible, inherit permissions from the parent site or use groups to manage permission settings for multiple users based on a specific role to minimize the number of individual permission settings that must be managed for each site, list, or library.

**Permission Settings on Individual Items**

SharePoint provides a granular permission management structure through sites, subsites, lists, and libraries to an individual document level. In what cases would managing permissions at the individual item level be warranted? How could this level of permission management be avoided?

## Set Up Versioning

**Document version history** is a feature of SharePoint libraries that retains copies of previously saved versions of files stored in the library. Using document version history in your SharePoint Online libraries can provide disaster recovery options for unexpected content changes.

Similar to shadow copies available on recent versions of Microsoft Windows, this feature allows for previous versions of files to be reviewed or restored when unintentional data changes or loss occur.

When establishing version history on a document library, it is necessary to determine what type of versions should be maintained and how many versions from history are necessary for storage and retrieval. The number of people collaborating on the individual files within the library can impact the choices made on both of these settings.

### Implementing File Versions

Mr. Mattingly has decided that due to the large number of contributors to the main documents library for the Painted Paradise Resort SharePoint site and the importance of the items stored in that library to the overall business operations of the resort, enabling version history on this library is necessary. He has decided that it is only necessary to keep a maximum of 10 major versions, but he thinks it is best to require users to check out the files for editing.

You will now set up version history on the main documents library for the Painted Paradise Resort SharePoint site with options to require check out and to maintain up to 10 major versions for each document file.

## sp01.26 To Set Up Version History on an Existing Library

a. Navigate to the Painted Paradise - First Last site, and click **Documents** in the Quick Launch.

b. On the LIBRARY tab, in the Settings group, click **Library Settings**.

c. Under the General Settings heading, click **Versioning settings**.

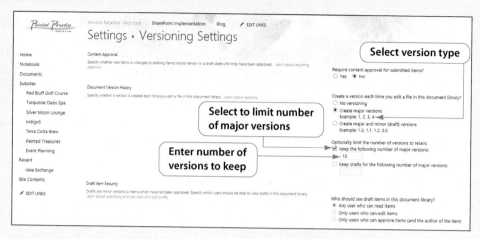

**Figure 24** Versioning Settings

d. Under **Document Version History**, click to select **Create major versions**.

e. Click to check the **Keep the following number of major versions** box, and then type 10 in the accompanying text box.

f. Under **Require Check Out**, click **Yes**, and then click **OK**.

---

**REAL WORLD ADVICE** | **Limit the Use of Version History**

Although the disaster recovery nature of versioning may encourage use on every document library, the storage costs associated with multiple copies of every document can cause performance issues. By default, libraries are set for no versioning to avoid these costs. Carefully consider the benefits and the number of versions needed for storage when implementing this feature.

---

**QUICK REFERENCE** | **Versioning Options on Document Libraries**

No versioning—This is the default setting, but it is not recommended if your document library contains business critical information.

Create major versions—Documents are numbered with whole numbers when the document is saved for the first time, when overwritten by a file of the same name, when checked-in after being checked out, when any properties of the document are changed, or when a previous version is restored.

Create major and minor (or draft) versions—Documents are numbered with whole numbers and decimals where the whole number represents major versions as described above, and decimal, or minor, versions are created at all other save points.

---

## Manage Workflows

**Workflows** are predefined sequences of tasks associated with items in libraries or lists. Workflows can be used to assign tasks to specific users, provide e-mail notification messages, and identify process status on new or modified items.

Two basic workflow types are built into SharePoint Server: disposition approval and three-state.

The **disposition approval workflow** manages document expiration and retention by allowing participants to decide whether to retain or delete expired documents.

The **three-state workflow** is used to track items in a list or library.

Additional custom workflows can be created for lists or libraries using Microsoft SharePoint Designer. Microsoft SharePoint Designer 2013 is a development tool for creating custom business solutions using SharePoint. It is available as a free download from the Microsoft Download Center web site.

### Defining Workflows

Mr. Matthews has decided that using a three-state workflow to track the status of the Implementation Requests created in the form library on the SharePoint Implementation site will help keep track of items that require attention. The workflow will be initiated by the creation of a new request in the library and set the status to Request Initiated; once reviewed, the status will be updated to Request Reviewed; and finally, once the request has been addressed, the status will be updated to Complete.

You will now define a three-state workflow for the Implementation Requests Form Library.

### sp01.27 To Define a Three-State Workflow on a Forms Library

a. Navigate to the SharePoint Implementation site, and then click on **Implementation Requests** in the Quick Launch.

b. On the LIBRARY tab, in the Manage Views group, click **Create Column**.

c. In the **Column name** box, type Status.

d. Click **Choice (menu to choose from)** under **The type of information in this column is**.

e. Click in the **Description** box, and type Workflow status.

f. In the Additional Column Settings section, select all text in the **Type each choice on a separate line** box, and then press Del.

g. Type Request Initiated. Press Enter. Type Request Reviewed. Press Enter. Type Complete.

h. Click **OK**.

i. On the LIBRARY tab, in the Settings group, click **Workflow Settings**, and then click **Add a Workflow**.

**SIDE NOTE**
**Choice Type Required**
The three-state workflow setup requires a column in the list that used the Choice type to update the status of the workflow throughout the process.

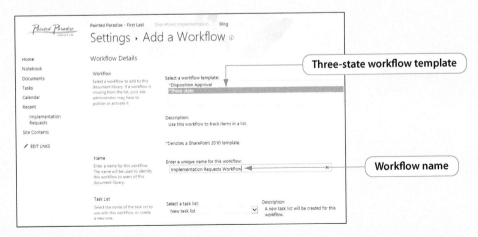

**Figure 25** Add a Workflow

j. In the **Select a workflow template** list, click **\*Three-state**.

k. In the **Enter a unique name for this workflow** box, type Implementation Requests Workflow.

l. In the Start Options section, click to check the **Creating a new item will start this workflow** box, and then click **Next**.

m. Click **OK**.

### Starting an Existing Workflow

Workflows can be started in several ways. They can be manually started by users with either Edit Item or Manage Lists permissions on the list or library associated with the workflow. They can be started automatically as part of the approval process for publishing of major versions of the list items. Finally, they can be started automatically when a new item is created or an existing item is changed.

You will now manually initiate the three-state workflow on the Implementation Requests Form Library.

**sp01.28 To Start a Workflow**

a. If necessary, navigate to the SharePoint Implementation site, and click **Implementation Requests** on the Quick Launch.

b. Click **Open Menu** ⋯ for the sp01ws01Request_LastFirst item.

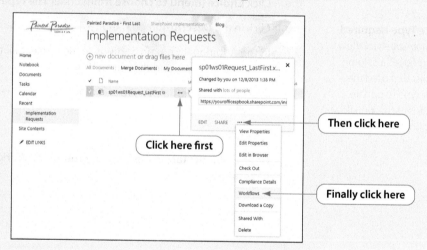

**Figure 26**   Open Menu Callout

c. Click **Open Menu** ⋯ in the callout, and then click **Workflows**.

d. Click **Implementation Requests Workflow**.

---

**CONSIDER THIS** | **Workflows in Business**

What documents exist in your place of employment that could benefit from the use of workflows? In what cases would workflows not be appropriate?

---

## Concept Check

1. In addition to the team site template, what are three site templates available in SharePoint?

2. What impact does changing the site theme have on a SharePoint site?

3. What is a Wiki page library used for in a SharePoint site?

4. Which common navigation features of SharePoint can contain links to additional pages in the Wiki page library?

5. What is the benefit of using groups when establishing site permissions?

6. What constitutes the creation of a major version in a document library with version history enabled?

7. What options exist for starting a workflow on a list or library?

## Key Terms

App   17
Blog template   7
Calendar app   18
Child site (subsite)   5
Community site template   7
Custom list   19
Discussion board   18
Disposition approval workflow   35
Document library   17
Document version history   33
Form library   17
Form template   25
Group   31

Library   17
List   17
Logo   14
Member   9
Microsoft InfoPath   25
Owner   9
Parent site   5
Permissions   31
Picture library   17
Project site template   7
Quick Launch   11
Ribbon   11
Site collection   4

Site template   7
Slide library   17
Team site template   7
Theme   14
Three-state workflow   35
Top-level team site   4
Top link bar   11
Top menu   11
User role   9
View   17
Visitor   9
Wiki page library   17
Workflow   34

## Visual Summary

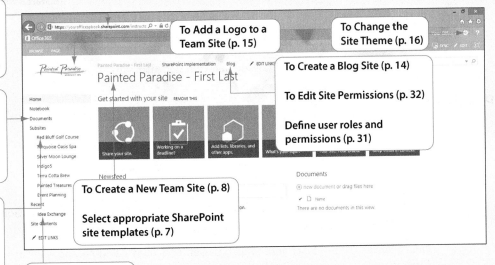

To Access SharePoint Server 2013 (p. 4)

To Select and Assign Group Permissions (p. 10)

To Set Up Version History on an Existing Library (p. 33)

Implement versioning options (p. 33)

To Create a Team Subsite (p. 12)

To Edit Homepage Content (p. 23)

To Add a Logo to a Team Site (p. 15)

To Change the Site Theme (p. 16)

To Create a Blog Site (p. 14)

To Edit Site Permissions (p. 32)

Define user roles and permissions (p. 31)

To Create a New Team Site (p. 8)

Select appropriate SharePoint site templates (p. 7)

To Add a Discussion Board (p. 18)

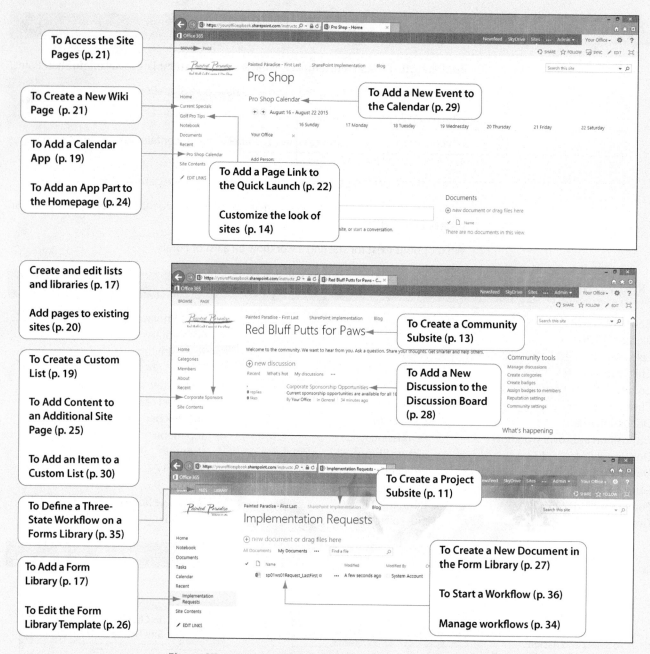

**To Access the Site Pages (p. 21)**

**To Create a New Wiki Page (p. 21)**

**To Add a Calendar App (p. 19)**

**To Add an App Part to the Homepage (p. 24)**

**To Add a New Event to the Calendar (p. 29)**

**To Add a Page Link to the Quick Launch (p. 22)**

**Customize the look of sites (p. 14)**

**Create and edit lists and libraries (p. 17)**

**Add pages to existing sites (p. 20)**

**To Create a Custom List (p. 19)**

**To Add Content to an Additional Site Page (p. 25)**

**To Add an Item to a Custom List (p. 30)**

**To Create a Community Subsite (p. 13)**

**To Add a New Discussion to the Discussion Board (p. 28)**

**To Define a Three-State Workflow on a Forms Library (p. 35)**

**To Create a Project Subsite (p. 11)**

**To Create a New Document in the Form Library (p. 27)**

**To Add a Form Library (p. 17)**

**To Edit the Form Library Template (p. 26)**

**To Start a Workflow (p. 36)**

**Manage workflows (p. 34)**

**Figure 27**   Collaboration through team sites

## Practice 1

**Student data file needed:**

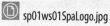 sp01ws01SpaLogo.jpg

**You will save your site as:**

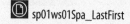 sp01ws01Spa_LastFirst

### Turquoise Oasis Spa Team Site

Production & Operations

Now that you have finished setting up the sites for Red Bluff Golf Club, Irene and Meda want to work with you to begin setting up the team site for the Turquoise Oasis Spa.

a.   Start your web browser, and then navigate and sign in to the SharePoint Team Site provided by your instructor.

b.   Click **Site Contents** in the Quick Launch, and then click **new subsite**.

c.   In the Title box, type Turquoise Oasis Spa - First Last.

d. In the URL box, delete any automatically generated text, then type sp01ws01Spa_ LastFirst.

e. Click **Use unique permissions** in the Permissions section.

f. Click **Yes** under Display this site on the Quick Launch of the parent site?, and then click **No** under Display this site on the top link bar of the parent site?.

g. Click **Create**, verify that names have been automatically assigned to the new members and owners groups, and then click **OK**.

h. Click **What's your style?** in the Get started with your site tiles at the top of the page, and then click the **Immerse** theme.

i. Click **Colors**, and then click **This palette is primarily Black with White and Green**.

j. Click **Site layout**, click **Seattle**, and then click **Try it out**.

k. Click **Yes, keep it**.

l. Click **Settings** ⚙, and then click **Site settings**.

m. Under the Look and Feel heading, click **Title, description, and logo**.

n. Under Insert Logo, click **FROM COMPUTER**.

o. In the Add a document dialog box, click **Browse**, locate and select the **sp01ws01SpaLogo** file in your student data files, click **Open**, and then click **OK** twice.

p. If necessary, click **Home** on the Quick Launch to return to the homepage, click **REMOVE THIS** next to the Get started with your site heading, and then click **OK**.

q. Click the **EDIT** button 🖉 on the Ribbon, and then click in the top placeholder.

r. On the FORMAT TEXT tab, in the Styles group, click **Heading 1**, type Turquoise Oasis Spa and then press ⏎ Enter .

s. Type Welcome to the Turquoise Oasis Spa - your relaxation destination. Explore the information throughout our site and contact us to schedule your next appointment.

t. Click **SAVE** 💾.

## Problem Solve 1

**Student data file needed:**

 sp01ps1Logo.jpg

**You will save your site as:**

sp01ps1Community_LastFirst

### Create a Community Site for the Painted Paradise Golf Resort and Spa

General Business

Mr. Mattingly decided that he wants to improve communication across the various areas of the entire resort and spa and has asked that you add a community site to the site collection to aid in these efforts.

a. Start your web browser, and then navigate and sign in to the SharePoint Team Site provided by your instructor.

b. Create a new Community Site subsite titled Another Day in Paradise with the URL sp01ps1Community_LastFirst.

c. Display this site on the Quick Launch of the parent site and use the top link bar from the parent site. Do not display the site on the top link bar of the parent site.

d. Navigate to the **Site Settings > Change the look** page, and apply the **Blossom** theme to the site.

e. Navigate to the **Site Settings** page, and then edit the **Title, description, and logo** site settings to insert the **sp01ps1Logo** file from your student data files.

f. If necessary, click **Home** in the Quick Launch to return to the homepage.

g. Add a new discussion to the community discussion board with the **Subject** Let's Talk - First Last and the **Body** This discussion board is a place for your ideas, comments, and suggestions for improvement at the Painted Paradise Resort and Spa. Click **Save**.

## Perform 1: Perform in Your Life

**Student data file needed:**
 None

**You will save your file as:**
 sp01pf1SiteMap_LastFirst.docx

**You will save your site as:**
sp01pf1School_LastFirst

Production & Operations

### Create a Site Collection for Your School

You have decided that SharePoint would be a great tool for managing the information needed by faculty and staff and have decided to design and build a site collection based on the main divisions and departments at your school.

a. Using the Microsoft Word desktop application, create a SmartArt graphic representing a site collection for your school based on the divisions, departments, and other communication needs perceived in the organization.

b. Save the document file using the name **sp01pf1SiteMap_LastFirst**.

c. Start your web browser, and then navigate and sign in to the SharePoint Team Site provided by your instructor.

d. Create a top-level team site with the **Title** Your School Name – First Last and the **URL** sp01pf1School_LastFirst.

e. Click **Use unique permissions** and display the site on the Quick Launch, but not the top link bar of the parent site.

f. Apply a theme to your site and remove the Get started with your site tiles.

g. Using the site map document you created, build the rest of the site collection using appropriate site templates for each of the outlined subsites in the hierarchy.

## WORKSHOP 2 | SHARE CONTENT IN ONEDRIVE FOR BUSINESS AND NEWSFEED

<br />

## OBJECTIVES

1. Identify differences between hierarchal and non-hierarchal file organization   p. 43

2. Use Word Online to create documents p. 50

3. Use Excel Online to create workbooks p. 54

4. Use PowerPoint Online to edit presentations p. 56

5. Use OneNote Online to create a notebook p. 61

6. Create and share a survey using Excel Online   p. 63

7. Share content using the Newsfeed   p. 68

8. Adjust privacy and notification settings for the Newsfeed   p. 74

### Prepare Case

General Business

## Sharing Content in OneDrive for Business and Newsfeed

After experiencing the benefits of SharePoint sites for centralizing content useful to the Red Bluff Golf Club staff and others at the Painted Paradise Golf Resort and Spa, Barry Cheney is interested in learning about the personal benefits of using OneDrive for Business, Office Online, and the Newsfeed available in SharePoint.

You will now help Barry organize his OneDrive for Business account, create and edit files using Office Online, and get familiar with how to use the Newsfeed for keeping up with people, sites, and content that are important to him.

© Andres Rodriguez/Fotolia

### REAL WORLD SUCCESS

"By storing my files on my OneDrive, I no longer have to carry around a USB drive or worry about not having access to my important business information on the go. The added benefit of Office Online also means that I can read, edit, and print my files from any computer, anywhere, even if Office isn't installed."

—Heather, alumnus and sales representative

**Student data files needed for this workshop:**

 sp01ws02EmployeeContacts.xlsx

 sp01ws02GolfLogo.jpg

 sp01ws02TournamentPresentation.pptx

**You will create folders as:**

 RBGC Records - First Last

 Bistro

 Pro Shop

 Putts for Paws

**You will save your files as:**

 sp01ws02Notebook_LastFirst

 sp01ws02Revenue_LastFirst.xlsx

 sp01ws02SponsorLetter_LastFirst.docx

 sp01ws02Survey_LastFirst.xlsx

 sp01ws02Tournament_LastFirst.pptx

# Organizing Your OneDrive for Business Storage

**OneDrive for Business** is a cloud storage location, included in SharePoint 2013, for personal organization of work-related documents. **Cloud storage** refers to the storage of data in an online location that is accessible across an Internet connection. Benefits to this type of storage include accessibility, centralized backup and recovery features, and sharing capabilities. OneDrive for Business is included in stand-alone installations of SharePoint Server 2013, SharePoint Online subscriptions, and subscriptions to Office 365.

Unlike the free personal storage OneDrive options available to anyone with a Microsoft or Outlook.com account, OneDrive for Business is intended for business purposes within your organization. OneDrive for Business is a good choice for storage when the document or file you are using is something that you only need to share with select users or keep for your own personal use. If the file is related to a team project or a larger audience is desired, it is better practice to store the file in a document library on a team site as appropriate.

## Access Your OneDrive for Business Storage

In order to access your OneDrive for Business storage, you must have a current account on a SharePoint server, SharePoint Online, or Office 365. In the top menu is a link simply named OneDrive. Your OneDrive for Business account is a SharePoint library created specifically for your use. Similar to other SharePoint libraries, you can organize the contents with folders, upload contents from your computer, or create new documents directly in the library using Office Online.

In addition, OneDrive for Business provides Quick Links to followed documents, documents shared with you, and recent documents. The **Followed Documents** link provides quick access to files throughout your organization's SharePoint sites and libraries. By following a document, you receive notifications in your newsfeed when someone updates the file or shares it with other people. Your decision to follow the document is shared with teammates as well. Based on what you choose to follow, additional documents will be suggested to follow.

The **Shared with Me** link provides access to any files that other users have shared with you from their OneDrive for Business accounts. Files stored in OneDrive for Business are private unless you decide to share them.

## Accessing Your OneDrive for Business Account

In order to help Mr. Cheney understand the structure of the OneDrive for Business account, you will demonstrate some of the navigation features of OneDrive for Business through your account. You will now access your SharePoint Server, sign in using your account, and access your personal OneDrive for Business storage.

**SIDE NOTE**

**Account Required**

An account on an established SharePoint Server is required to complete the steps in this activity.

### sp02.00 To Access Your Personal OneDrive for Business Account

a. Start your web browser, and then navigate to the SharePoint Server provided by your instructor.

b. If prompted, type your username and your password, and then click **Sign in**.

c. From the top menu, click **OneDrive**.

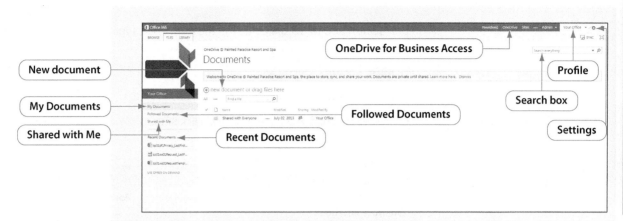

**New document**

**My Documents**

**Shared with Me**

**OneDrive for Business Access**

**Profile**

**Search box**

**Settings**

**Followed Documents**

**Recent Documents**

**Figure 1**  Sample OneDrive for Business account

d.  On the Quick Launch, click **Followed Documents**.

e.  On the Quick Launch, click **Shared with Me**.

f.  On the Quick Launch, click **My Documents**.

## Organize Files in a Hierarchal Structure

A traditional approach to organizing files is to use a **hierarchal structure** that consists of folders and subfolders containing related files. In the same way that sites and subsites were created in the first workshop, organizing files in your OneDrive for Business account using a hierarchal structure can be developed using a top-down approach of creating the top-level folders and then building subfolders within as appropriate.

As a convenient tool for quickly sharing files with all users in your organization, your OneDrive for Business account contains an initial folder named Shared with Everyone. Any content placed in this folder is shared with everyone in your organization, so use caution when adding items to this folder and consider available libraries on existing SharePoint sites as an alternative for team-specific document storage.

### Creating Folders to Store Files

Creating additional folders in your OneDrive for Business account can follow any organization method that you desire for structuring your content. Folders can be based on projects, document types, dates, and more. If you use a traditional filing system for organizing paper files, its structure can be emulated in the electronic storage.

Because the OneDrive for Business account is a personal file storage location in SharePoint, the organization of the folders and files does not have to meet the needs of other team members or the organization as a whole; however, it should have some defined structure to make it easier to share files or to locate them later.

You will now create a folder structure on your OneDrive for storing documents related to the Red Bluff Golf Club.

### sp02.01 **To Create a Folder**

a.  If necessary, click **OneDrive** on the top menu, and then click **My Documents** on the Quick Launch.

b.  Click the **FILES** tab, in the New group, click **New Folder**.

c.  In the Create a new folder dialog box, in the **Name** box, type RBGC Records - First Last, using your first and last name, and then click **Save**.

d.  Click **RBGC Records – First Last**.

e.  Click **new document**, and then click **New folder**.

f.  In the **Name** box, type Pro Shop, and then click **Save**.

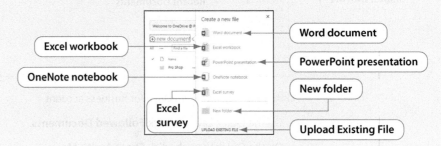

**Figure 2**   New document callout

g.  Click **new document**, and then click **New folder**.

h.  In the **Name** box, type Bistro, and then click **Save**.

i.  Click **new document**, and then click **New folder**.

j.  In the **Name** box, type Putts for Paws, and then click **Save**.


### Uploading Files to OneDrive

When transitioning to a cloud storage option, such as OneDrive for Business it would be inefficient and time-consuming to recreate files housed in traditional storage locations, such as computer hard drives and network locations. OneDrive for Business provides multiple options for uploading existing content to your account on the SharePoint server.

For individual files, the Upload Document option on the FILES tab of the Ribbon or the Upload Existing File option at the bottom of the new document callout opens the Add a document dialog box to browse for the file on your computer.

For multiple files or folders, the option to upload files using File Explorer through traditional copy or move file management tasks is available through a link in the Add a document dialog box or in the Connect & Export group on the LIBRARY tab of the Ribbon.

Individual or multiple files and folders can also be added to the OneDrive by dragging the content from File Explorer into the OneDrive for Business page in the web browser.

You will now explore options for uploading content from your student data files to your OneDrive for Business account.


### sp02.02 To Upload a File to OneDrive for Business

a.  If necessary, click **OneDrive** on the top menu, click **My Documents** in the Quick Launch, and then click **RBGC Records - First Last**.

b.  On the FILES tab, in the New group, click **Upload Document**.

c.  In the Add a document dialog box, click **Browse**, and then select the **sp01ws02EmployeeContacts** file from your student data files.

**Figure 3**    Add a document dialog box

d.  Click **Open**, and then click **OK**.

e.  Click **Putts for Paws**, click **new document**, and then click **UPLOAD EXISTING FILE**.

f.  In the Add a document dialog box, click **Browse**, and then select the **sp01ws02TournamentPresentation** file from your student data files.

g.  Click **Open**, and then click **OK**.

## Organize Files with Tags and Notes

A modern approach to file management is the use of tags and notes to organize content in various folders throughout your OneDrive for Business account. **Tags** are used to classify and remember pages, documents, or external sites in SharePoint. **Notes** are used to comment on pages, documents, and external sites.

Tags and notes are stored on the item where they are applied and listed under your profile for easy retrieval. Any tags or notes associated with files can be viewed by other people with access to the file; however, you can mark a tag as private to prevent others from seeing that you tagged the item.

### Adding Tags and Notes to a File

Adding tags or notes to a file is a two-step process requiring first the selection of the file in the folder where it is stored, and second the actual application of appropriate tags and note content. You will now add tags and notes to the files uploaded during the previous activity.

sp02.03 **To Add Tags or Notes to a File**

a.  If necessary, navigate to the **Putts for Paws** subfolder in the RBGC Records - First Last folder on your OneDrive for Business account.

b.  Click in the blank space to the left of **sp01ws02TournamentPresentation** to select the file and add a check mark in the blank column.

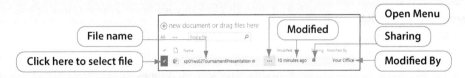

**Figure 4**    Selecting a file in OneDrive for Business

c.  On the FILES tab, in the Tags and Notes group, click **Tags & Notes**.

d.  On the TAGS tab of the Tags and Note Board dialog box, under the My Tags heading, click the tags box.

e. Type charity;presentation;tournament;fundraising and then click **Save**.

f. Click the **NOTE BOARD** tab, and then click the notes box.

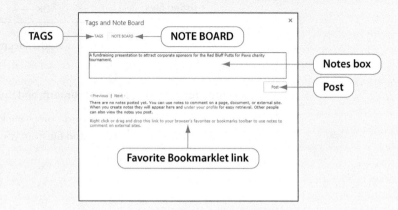

**Figure 5** Tags and Note Board dialog box

g. Type A fundraising presentation to attract corporate sponsors for the Red Bluff Putts for Paws charity tournament. and then click **Post**.

h. Close the Tags and Note Board dialog box.

### Tagging an External Site

In order to collect and organize external sites with tags and notes in your OneDrive for Business account, SharePoint provides a **bookmarklet**, or a link that is added to the web browser's favorites or bookmarks toolbar to run a script that sends information to sites on the Internet. The bookmarklet is available in the Tags & Notes dialog box for the My Documents library or on the Tags and Notes page of your profile.

Mr. Cheney wants to store links to the web sales and customer supplier reports from the Red Bluff Golf Club page of the Painted Paradise Golf Resort and Spa website in his OneDrive for Business account with specific tags. You will now use the bookmarklet to tag each of these pages in your OneDrive for Business account.

### sp02.04 To Add Tags to an External Site

a. Click **OneDrive** on the top menu, and then click **RBGC Records - First Last**.

b. On the LIBRARY tab, in the Tags and Notes group, click **Tags & Notes**.

c. On the TAGS tab of the OneDrive for Business dialog box, right-click **Right click or drag and drop this link to your browser's favorites or bookmarks toolbar to tag external sites.**, and then click **Add to favorites**.

d. In the Add a Favorite dialog box, click **Add**.

e. Close the OneDrive for Business dialog box.

f. In the address bar, type www.paintedparadiseresort.com/Red_Bluff_Web.htm and then press [Enter].

g. Click **Web Sales Report 2010**.

## SIDE NOTE
**Separating Tags**
Tags can be separated with commas or semicolons; however, the tags box will automatically replace commas with semicolons as a standard.

## SIDE NOTE
**Favorite Bookmarklet**
The bookmarklet only needs to be added to your favorites list once. It can be used with any external websites in the future.

h. With the Red Bluff Golf Club – Web Sales Report page displayed in the browser, click the **Tags and Note Board** link in your Favorites list.

i. On the TAGS tab of the Tags and Note Board window, click in the tags box, type web sales;2010;report, and then click **Save**.

j. Close the Tags and Note Board window, and then click the **Back** button 🔙 in your web browser.

k. Click **Customer Supplier Report 2013**.

l. With the Customer: Red Bluff Golf Club - Supplier Report page displayed in the browser, click the **Tags and Note Board** link in your Favorites list.

m. On the TAGS tab of the Tags and Note Board window, click in the tags box, type customer;supplier report;2013, and then click **Save**.

n. Close the Tags and Note Board window.

---

**CONSIDER THIS** | **Benefits to Organizing with Tags and Notes**

What are some reasons that tags and notes are used for organizing content in cloud storage locations? What are some places other than SharePoint that you have seen tags and notes used to organize content?

---

**REAL WORLD ADVICE** | **Use a Combination of Hierarchal and Non-Hierarchal Organization**

It is recommended that you use a combination of hierarchal and non-hierarchal organization in your OneDrive for Business account as each method has unique benefits. The hierarchal approach is useful for grouping related files, while the non-hierarchal approach allows for quickly locating files by subject or purpose when the physical storage location is not known.

## Manage Existing Files and Folders

OneDrive for Business provides a variety of tools for managing files and folders including editing properties, deleting, sharing or following items, and setting alerts.

Sharing a file or folder allows other users within the organization access to view or edit the contents. A file can be shared through an invitation through SharePoint that can include an optional e-mail invitation. The required sign-in option on the invitation can control access to the file based on authenticated users. Alternatively, you can generate a link for view only or edit capabilities that can be shared via e-mail, posted on a website, or otherwise distributed to anyone who needs access to the file.

By following a document, you receive notifications in your newsfeed when someone updates the file or shares it with other people. Your decision to follow the document is shared with teammates as well. Based on what you choose to follow, additional documents will be suggested to follow.

### Editing Item Properties

Properties that can be edited on files are the file name and title. On folders, the only property that can be edited is the name. You will now rename one of the uploaded files in the OneDrive to reflect your name.

**To Edit Properties on a Document in OneDrive for Business**

a. In your web browser, navigate to your OneDrive for Business account.

b. Click **RBGC Records – First Last**, and then click **Putts for Paws**.

c. Click the **Open Menu** button ⋯ to the right of **sp01ws02TournamentPresentation**, click the **Open Menu** button ⋯ at the bottom of the callout, and then click **Edit Properties**.

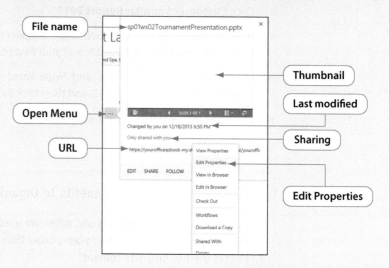

**Figure 6**   Item properties callout and menu

d. Select the existing text in the **Name** box, press ⌷Del⌷, and then type sp01ws02Tournament_LastFirst, using your last and first name.

e. Select the existing text in the **Title** box, press ⌷Del⌷, and then type Red Bluff Putts for Paws Corporate Sponsor Presentation.

f. Click **Save**.

### Sharing Files and Folders

Sharing a file or folder allows other users within the organization access to view or edit the contents. Mr. Cheney has decided that select individuals will need access to the files in the Red Bluff Golf Club folder added to the OneDrive for Business account, but he wants to be sure that only select authenticated users have access to the files and that none of them is able to modify the contents of any files except sp01ws02Tournament_LastFirst.

You will now provide your instructor with view only access to the Red Bluff Golf Club folder on your OneDrive for Business account and share the sp01ws02Tournament_LastFirst file with edit capability.

**To Share a Folder with Other Users**

a. Click **My Documents** in the Quick Launch, click the **Open Menu** button ⋯ to the right of **RBGC Records - First Last**, and then click **SHARE**.

**Enter instructor e-mail here**

**Set sharing option**

**Include optional personal message**

**Share**

**Cancel**

**Figure 7** Share 'RBGC Records - First Last' dialog box

b. Click the **Enter names, email addresses, or 'Everyone'.** box, and then type your instructor's e-mail address.

c. Click **Can edit**, then click **Can view**, and then click **Share**.

d. Click **RBGC Records - First Last**, and then click **Putts for Paws**.

e. Click the **Open Menu** button [...] to the right of **sp01ws02Tournament_LastFirst**, and then click **SHARE**.

f. Click the **Enter names, email addresses, or 'Everyone'.** box, type your instructor's e-mail address, and then click **Share**.

### Setting Alerts on Files

Setting an alert on a file or folder generates e-mail or text messages immediately or in summary format on specific days and times when changes are made to the item. In order to keep track of any changes made to the sp01ws02Tournament_LastFirst file, you will now add an alert that sends an e-mail immediately whenever someone else changes the file.

### sp02.07 To Set an Alert on a File in OneDrive for Business

a. If necessary, navigate to the Putts for Paws subfolder and select the **sp01ws02Tournament_LastFirst** file.

b. On the FILES tab, in the Share & Track group, click **Alert Me**, and then click **Set alert on this document**.

c. Click below the **Users** heading and then type your e-mail address.

> **Troubleshooting**
> A valid e-mail address must be entered or an account name with an associated e-mail address to successfully setup e-mail alert options. If an error appears related to your profile e-mail address, close the message window and update your profile to include a valid e-mail address.

d. Under the **Send me an alert when** heading, click **Someone else changes a document**, and then click **OK**.

Delivery Method—Alerts can be sent by e-mail or text message (SMS).

Send Alerts for These Changes—Alerts can be sent when anything changes, someone else changes a document, someone else changes a document created by me, or someone else changes a document last modified by me.

When to Send Alerts—Alerts can be sent immediately, in a daily summary, or in a weekly summary format.

The sync feature of OneDrive for Business allows users to sync their OneDrive for Business content with their local computer, ensuring that content on the OneDrive is always available, even when the user does not have access to the Internet. Changes made offline are synced when an Internet connection becomes available.

## Using Office Online

**Office Online** is the set of online companions to Word, Excel, PowerPoint, and OneNote. If you work on a computer without the desktop applications installed, Office Online allows for the creation and editing of files stored in OneDrive for Business or in document libraries on SharePoint team sites. Changes to files open in Office Online are automatically saved.

In this next section, you will explore Office Online available in OneDrive for Business.

## Create Documents in Word Online

**Word Online** provides the core functionality of Microsoft Word for viewing, printing, and editing Word documents in the browser. The familiar Ribbon interface from Microsoft Word is simplified when editing a document in the browser to only include the FILE, HOME, INSERT, PAGE LAYOUT, VIEW, and REVIEW tabs.

The FILE tab includes the ability to save a copy, print, share, and close the document. It also includes an option to **Open in Word**, which opens the document in the Word desktop application, if installed on the computer, for full functionality and editing features.

The HOME tab contains the most commonly used commands, including font and paragraph formatting, styles, Clipboard tools, and Find and Replace buttons.

The INSERT tab includes commands for inserting page breaks, tables, pictures, clip art, links, header and footer content, and page numbers.

The PAGE LAYOUT tab includes commands for page settings of margins, orientation, and size, as well as paragraph indentation and spacing options.

The VIEW tab allows for switching between editing and reading views or for editing the header and footer. The **Editing view** of Word Online is the view that allows for modification of file contents, and use of the editing tools on the Ribbon. This view simplifies the display of the document and uses placeholders for content that cannot be edited in the browser. The **Reading view** shows the document as it will appear in the full application or in print form with options to print and share the document, to search for content, or to add or review comments.

The REVIEW tab contains commands for checking spelling and creating and reviewing comments.

### Creating a New Word Document

To create a new Word document using Word Online, you will select the Word document option from the Create a new file callout from the new document button in any folder on your OneDrive for Business account. When creating the file, you will be prompted only for a file name and the new document will be saved in the current folder on the drive.

You will now create a donation request letter for the upcoming Red Bluff Putts for Paws charity tournament that Mr. Cheney can send to potential corporate sponsors.

### sp02.08 To Create a New Word Document

a. If necessary, navigate to the Putts for Paws subfolder on your OneDrive for Business account.

b. Click **new document**, and then click **Word document**.

c. In the Create a new document dialog box, click in the **Document Name** box, and then type sp01ws02SponsorLetter_LastFirst, using your last and first name.

d. Click **OK**.

e. In Word Online, type The Red Bluff Golf Club at the Painted Paradise Resort and Spa is proud to be hosting our annual Red Bluff Putts for Paws charity tournament next month., press Enter, and then type As a valued member of the local business community I would like to personally offer you an opportunity to be a corporate sponsor at the event. Sponsorships are limited to the first twenty responses to this opportunity including: all 18 holes, the reception, and the silent auction.

f. Press Enter, then type I look forward to your response in the near future., press Enter, type Sincerely,, press Enter, and then type Mr. Barry Cheney.

### Inserting Pictures and Clip Art

Pictures and clip art can be used to enhance the visual appeal of a document. **Pictures** are image files stored on your computer that can be uploaded for use in the document. **Clip Art** is a searchable collection of royalty-free images provided by Microsoft for insertion in the document.

Once inserted in the document, the contextual PICTURE TOOLS FORMAT tab can be used to add picture styles or to adjust or resize the image. You will now add the Red Bluff Golf Course & Pro Shop logo and an appropriate clip art image to the request letter.

### sp02.09 To Insert Images and Clip Art

a. If necessary, open the **sp01ws02SponsorLetter_LastFirst** document from your Putts for Paws subfolder on OneDrive for Business.

b. Click at the beginning of the first paragraph in the letter, press Enter, and then click in the blank line at the top of the letter.

c. On the HOME tab, in the Paragraph group, click **Center**.

d. On the INSERT tab, in the Pictures group, click **Picture**.

e. In the Choose File to Upload dialog box, browse to your student data files, select **sp01ws02GolfLogo**, and then click **Open**.

f. Click at the end of the second text paragraph in the letter, and then press Enter.

g. On the HOME tab, in the Paragraph group, click **Center**.

h. On the INSERT tab, in the Pictures group, click **Clip Art**.

i. In the Insert Clip Art dialog box, click in the Search box, type golf course, and then press Enter.

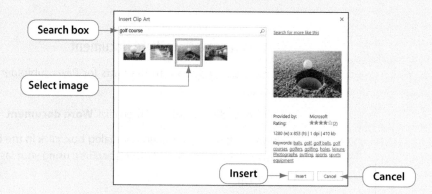

**Figure 8**   Insert Clip Art dialog box

j. Click the image matching the figure above in the Insert Clip Art dialog box, and then click **Insert**.

> **Troubleshooting**
> If the displayed clip art image is not available, select a similar image from the Insert Clip Art dialog box, and then click Insert.

### Using Reading View to Insert Comments

The Reading view of Word Online allows for the creation, review, and response to comments throughout the document. Comments in Word Online can only be created on text content in the document or in response to existing comments in the document that were applied in the Word desktop app.

You will now preview your letter in the Reading view and add a new comment to the document using Word Online.

### sp02.10 To Insert Comments Using Reading View

a. If necessary, open the **sp01ws02SponsorLetter_LastFirst** document from your Putts for Paws subfolder on OneDrive for Business.

b. On the VIEW tab, in the Document Views group, click **Reading View**.

c. On the Ribbon, click **COMMENTS**.

d. Click at the end of the second text paragraph, and then in the Comments pane, click **New Comment**.

**SIDE NOTE**

**Selecting Content**

The Reading view does not allow for selection of individual words or images for commenting. Lines and paragraphs are automatically selected.

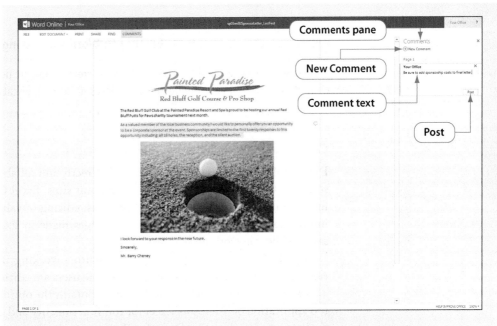

**Figure 9**   Reading View with Comments pane

e. Type **Be sure to add sponsorship costs to final letter.**, and then click **Post**.

f. Close the Comments pane.

## Printing from and Exiting Word Online

In order to eliminate layout discrepancies due to browser differences and print settings related to web pages, documents printed from Word Online are printed to a PDF file and can be sent to the printer or saved from the PDF version.

Changes to the open document are automatically saved when using Word Online. When finished reviewing or editing a document, simply exiting the app will return to the OneDrive for Business folder. You will now print a copy of your document and exit Word Online.

### sp02.11 To Print from and Exit Word Online

a. If necessary, open the **sp01ws02SponsorLetter_LastFirst** document from your Putts for Paws subfolder on OneDrive for Business.

b. On the FILE tab, click **Print**, and then click **Print to PDF**.

c. In the Microsoft Word Online dialog box, click **Click here to view the PDF of your document.**

> **Troubleshooting**
> If prompted by the web browser software to Open or Save the created PDF file, click Open. A reader software application for PDF files is required to open the file.

d. Save or print a copy of the PDF from your reader software, and then close the reader application.

e. Return to the web browser, and in the Microsoft Word Online dialog box, click **Close**.

f. On the FILE tab, click **Exit**.

## Create Workbooks in Excel Online

**Excel Online** provides the ability to work directly and collaboratively on Excel workbooks stored in OneDrive for Business or SharePoint sites. Excel Online supports viewing and interacting with data in existing worksheets, editing of values and formulas, and inserting of tables, hyperlinks, and charts. Changes made in Excel Online are automatically saved while you work on it.

Excel Online also supports multiple editors working in the workbook at the same time. The status bar indicates when multiple users are editing the document.

Similar to Word Online, Excel Online contains the option to open the file in the desktop application of Microsoft Excel for full functionality and changes made in the application are saved back to OneDrive for Business or the document library in SharePoint.

### Creating a New Excel Workbook

In the same way that a new Word document is created using Word Online. you create new Excel workbooks directly in your OneDrive for Business account by selecting the Excel workbook option from the Create a new file callout from the new document button in any folder on your OneDrive for Business account. When creating the file, you will be prompted only for a file name and the new workbook will be saved in the current folder on the drive.

Mr. Cheney is interested in recording and charting the revenue sources for the Red Bluff Golf Course & Pro Shop over the past year. You will now create a new workbook and enter the appropriate data for the year.

### sp02.12 To Create a New Excel Workbook

a. In your web browser, navigate to the **RBGC Records - First Last** folder on your OneDrive for Business account.

b. Click **new document**, and then click **Excel workbook**.

c. In the Create a new document dialog box, click in the **Document Name** box, type sp01ws02Revenue_LastFirst, and then click **OK**.

d. In Excel Online with cell **A1** active, type Red Bluff Golf Course and Pro Shop Revenue Sources and then press Enter.

e. Click cell **B2**, type Quarter 1 and then press Tab.

f. Click cell **B2**, and then drag the fill handle to cell **E2**.

g. Click cell **F2**, and then type Total.

h. Click cell **A3**, type Membership, and then press Enter.

i. In cells **A4:A8**, type the following, pressing Enter after each: Rentals, Lessons, Events, Product Sales, and Total.

j. In cells **B3:E7**, type the values in the table below.

|              | Quarter 1 | Quarter 2 | Quarter 3 | Quarter 4 |
|--------------|-----------|-----------|-----------|-----------|
| Membership   | 257000    | 375000    | 315000    | 279000    |
| Rentals      | 9000      | 15000     | 12000     | 8500      |
| Lessons      | 10550     | 36000     | 34350     | 10250     |
| Events       | 18000     | 42000     | 37500     | 21000     |
| Product Sales | 212750   | 407653    | 394180    | 463796    |

**Table 1**  Worksheet data

k.  Click cell **F3**, then on the HOME tab, in the Editing group, click **AutoSum**, and then press ⎯Enter⎯.

l.  Click cell **F3**, and then drag the fill handle to cell **F7**.

m.  Click cell **B8**, then on the HOME tab, in the Editing group, click **AutoSum**, and then press ⎯Enter⎯.

n.  Click cell **B8**, and then drag the fill handle to cell **F8**.

o.  Click between column indicators **A** and **B** and drag the right border of column A to the right until all text in cells **A3:A7** is visible in the worksheet.

p.  Select **B3:F3**; then on the HOME tab, in the Number group, click **Number Format**, and then click **Accounting**.

q.  Select **B4:F7**; then on the HOME tab, in the Number group, click **Comma Style**.

r.  Select **B8:F8**; then on the HOME tab, in the Number group, click **Number Format**, and then click **Accounting**.

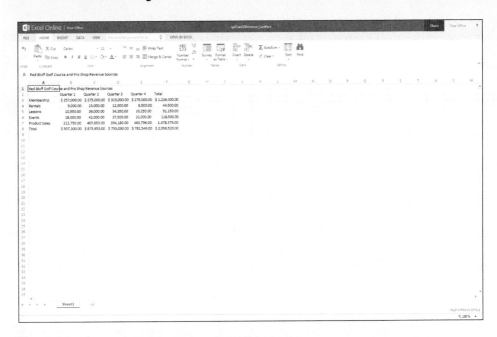

**Figure 10**  Red Bluff Revenue Sources worksheet

s.  Click cell **A1**, and then verify that your worksheet matches the figure above.

### Charting Excel Data

Excel Online supports a large selection of the common chart types available in the Excel desktop application for creation directly in the web browser. On the INSERT tab, in the Charts group, you can choose from Column, Line, Pie, Bar, Area, Scatter, and Radar chart types.

The type of chart you use in a workbook is determined by the structure of the data that will be represented and the desired visual result. In general, pie charts should be used to represent a single series of data with associated labels. Bar, column, and line charts, in contrast, are effective for representing multiple series of data. Bar and column charts are useful for side by side comparison, while line charts illustrate a connection or transition between data points.

You will now add a column chart to your workbook to visually represent the various revenue sources over the past year.

### sp02.13 To Insert a Chart

a. If necessary, open the **sp01ws02Revenue_LastFirst** workbook from your RBGC Records - First Last folder on your OneDrive for Business account.

b. Select **A2:E7**; then on the INSERT tab, in the Charts group, click **Column**, and then click **Clustered Column**.

c. Drag the chart object below the data on the worksheet, and then use the sizing handles to resize the chart, approximately filling the range A10:F21.

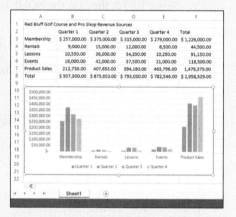

**Figure 11**    Red Bluff Revenue Sources worksheet with chart

d. On the FILE tab, click **Exit**.

## Create Presentations in PowerPoint Online

**PowerPoint Online** supports the viewing, editing, and printing of PowerPoint presentations from within the web browser. Although themes, transitions, and animation effects applied in the desktop application of PowerPoint will be maintained in existing presentations opened with PowerPoint Online. a limited set of theme, transition, and animation effects are available for application within the online version when creating or editing a presentation in the browser.

In **Slide Show view**, the presentation is displayed full-screen, allowing presentation directly from the web browser. One limitation compared to the full version of PowerPoint is that the online version does not support the playback of audio or video content in the presentations.

As with the other Office Online apps, changes made to PowerPoint presentations using the online version are automatically saved, so use Undo to get rid of changes you do not want to keep before closing the file. For full functionality or to support audio and video playback, simply click Open in PowerPoint from the FILE tab.

### Editing a Presentation in PowerPoint Online

Clicking on an existing presentation link in your OneDrive for Business account will open the presentation in Reading view within the web browser. The Reading view provides a preview of slide contents and related notes, with the option to share the presentation, or to create, review, and respond to comments. To make edits to the content or structure of the presentation, the presentation must be switched to Editing view.

You will now open the existing sp01ws02Tournament_LastFirst presentation file, uploaded to your OneDrive for Business account and renamed in earlier activities, and help Mr. Cheney complete the creation of the presentation.

### sp02.14 To Edit an Existing PowerPoint Presentation

a. In your web browser, navigate to the **Putts for Paws** subfolder on your OneDrive for Business account.

b. Click **sp01ws02Tournament_LastFirst**.

c. On the Ribbon, click **EDIT PRESENTATION**, and then click **Edit in PowerPoint Online**.

d. Click **Click to add title**, and then type Red Bluff Putts for Paws.

e. Click **Click to add subtitle**, and then type Corporate Sponsorship Opportunities.

### Applying Themes and Variants

A limited set of presentation themes and design variants are available in PowerPoint Online. **Themes** provide a visual structure to the presentation, including colors, fonts, effects, background styles, and placeholder positioning. **Variants** provide alternative options for the base theme with modifications to colors, fonts, or effects.

Themes and variants are applied consistently to all slides in the presentation from the DESIGN tab of the Ribbon. You will now apply a theme and variant to the current presentation.

### sp02.15 To Apply a Presentation Theme and Variant

a. If necessary, open the **sp01ws02Tournament_LastFirst** file from your Putts for Paws subfolder on your OneDrive for Business account for editing in PowerPoint Online.

b. On the DESIGN tab, in the Themes group, click **Ion Boardroom**.

Ion Boardroom theme

**Figure 12**   Presentation themes and variants

c. On the DESIGN tab, in the Variants group, click **Variant 4**.

### Inserting Slides

Additional slides should be added to the presentation as necessary for each main point. PowerPoint Online requires the selection of a slide layout when inserting new slides into a presentation. A **slide layout** designates the number, location, and related content association of placeholders on the slide. You will now create an additional slide in the current presentation.

SIDE NOTE
**New Slide Options**
The New Slide button is available on both the HOME and INSERT tabs of the Ribbon in PowerPoint Online.

### sp02.16 **To Add Slides to a Presentation**

a.  If necessary, open the **sp01ws02Tournament_LastFirst** file from your Putts for Paws subfolder on your OneDrive for Business account for editing in PowerPoint Online.

b.  On the HOME tab, in the Slides group, click **New Slide**.

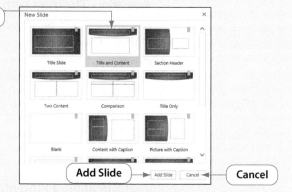

Title and Content layout

Add Slide

Cancel

**Figure 13**    New Slide dialog box

c.  In the New Slide dialog box, click **Title and Content**, and then click **Add Slide**.

d.  Click **Click to add title**, and then type Sponsorship Opportunities.

e.  Click **Click to add text**, type 20 opportunities available, and then press Enter.

f.  Press Tab, type All 18 holes on the Red Bluff Golf Course, and then press Enter.

g.  Type Catered reception after the tournament, press Enter, and then type Silent auction during the tournament.

## Changing Slide Layouts

Once a slide is created, if a different slide layout is determined to be more appropriate for the slide contents, the layout can be easily changed to one of the other options. Any entered text or contents in existing placeholders will be automatically moved into the appropriate placeholders in the new layout. You will now change the layout of an existing slide in the current presentation.

### sp02.17 To Change a Slide Layout

a. If necessary, open the **sp01ws02Tournament_LastFirst** file from your Putts for Paws subfolder on your OneDrive for Business account for editing in PowerPoint Online.

b. Click slide 2 in the Slides pane, and then on the HOME tab, in the Slides group, click **Layout**.

c. In the Slide Layout dialog box, click **Two Content**, and then click **Change Layout**.

d. On the INSERT tab, in the Images group, click **Clip Art**.

e. In the Clip Art dialog box **search** box, type golf club, and then press Enter.

**Figure 14**  Clip Art dialog box

f. Click the animated image of the man swinging a golf club shown in the figure above, and then click **Insert**.

g. Resize and move the image to fill most of the right side of the slide.

---

| QUICK REFERENCE | Available Slide Layouts |
| --- | --- |

Fifteen slide layouts are available in PowerPoint Online:

- Title Slide
- Title and Content
- Section Header
- Two Content
- Comparison
- Title Only
- Blank
- Content with Caption

- Picture with Caption
- Panoramic Picture with Caption
- Title and Caption
- Quote with Caption
- Name Card
- 3 Column
- 3 Picture Column

### Inserting Notes and Comments

**Notes** are added to individual slides in a PowerPoint presentation to record content that is shared verbally, but not included on the displayed slide. Notes are entered in the **Notes pane** that displays below the current slide in the Editing view of the presentation in PowerPoint Online.

**Comments** are a feedback feature of PowerPoint Online that allow multiple users to discuss the presentation with direct connection to the slide content. Comments can be added in the Editing view of the presentation and are visible in either the Editing or Reading views.

You will now add notes and comments to the current presentation.

---

**sp02.18 To Insert Notes and Comments**

a. If necessary, open the **sp01ws02Tournament_LastFirst** file from your Putts for Paws subfolder on your OneDrive for Business account for editing in PowerPoint Online and display Slide 2.

b. Click in the Notes pane designated by **Click to add notes**.

> **Troubleshooting**
>
> If the Notes pane is not visible, on the VIEW tab, in the Show group, click Notes.

c. Type Sponsorship opportunities are limited to the first twenty corporate sponsors.

d. On the VIEW tab, in the Show group, click **Show Comments**.

e. Click at the end of the first bullet in the content placeholder, and then in the Comments pane, click **NEW**.

f. Type Should we include prices on this slide?, and then press Enter.

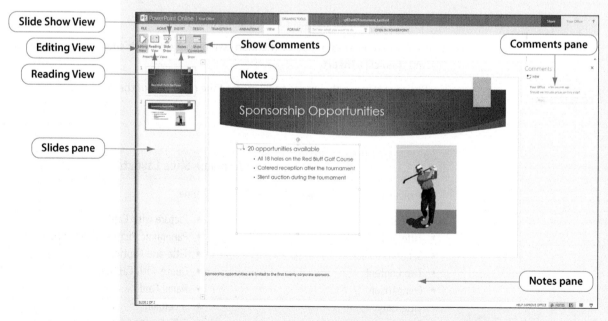

**Figure 15**   Slide 2 with Notes and Comments panes

### Viewing a Slide Show

In Slide Show view, the presentation is displayed full-screen, allowing presentation directly from the web browser. When you are viewing the presentation in Slide Show view, controls for navigating to the previous or next slide and for ending the show are located in the bottom left corner of the slide, becoming visible when the mouse cursor is moved to that corner of the screen.

Alternatively, when navigating through the presentation in Slide Show view, advancement in sequence through the slides can be done with a mouse click, the Spacebar, the ⬇ key, or the ➡ key.

Returning to the previous slide can be done with the ⬅ key, ⬆ key, or by right-clicking on the active slide and clicking the Previous menu option. To go to a specific slide in the presentation, right-click on the active slide and click Go to Slide, provide the slide number in the dialog box, and then click OK.

Ending the show at any time can be done with the End Show button in the bottom-left corner of the slide or by right-clicking on the slide and clicking the End Show menu option.

You will now use the Slide Show view to preview the entire presentation.

### sp02.19 To View a Slide Show

a.  If necessary, open the **sp01ws02Tournament_LastFirst** file from your Putts for Paws subfolder on your OneDrive for Business account for editing in PowerPoint Online.

b.  On the VIEW tab, in the Presentation Views group, click **Slide Show**.

c.  Click through the presentation, and at the end of the slide show, click to exit.

d.  Click **FILE**, and then click **Exit**.

> **Troubleshooting**
> If presented with a warning that the web page you are viewing is trying to close the window, click Yes.

## Create Notebooks in OneNote Online

**OneNote Online** provides access to electronic notebooks that make it easy to store, organize, and share a variety of content in a single location online. OneNote Online supports simultaneous efforts from multiple users and keeps track of who made which changes to the notebook pages.

With the ability to insert text, tables, pictures, clip art, and hyperlinks, OneNote Online can collect all of the pieces of a larger project for review and discussion in a single file. In support of multiple users and collaborative efforts, OneNote Online automatically saves changes as they occur and keeps a history of page versions, allowing for the review of what changes were made or to restore previous versions if necessary.

### Creating a New OneNote Notebook

OneNote notebooks can be created for a wide variety of purposes. Notebooks are organized into one or more sections, each containing one or more pages of related content. A new OneNote notebook can be created directly in OneDrive for Business by selecting the OneNote notebook option from the Create a new file callout from the new document button in any folder on your OneDrive for Business account. You will now create a new notebook for Mr. Cheney to collect information on the various business elements of the Red Bluff Golf Course & Pro Shop.

a. In your web browser, navigate to the **RBGC Records - First Last** folder on your OneDrive for Business account.

b. Click **new document**, and then click **OneNote notebook**.

c. In the Create a new document dialog box, click the **Document Name** box, type sp01ws02Notebook_LastFirst, using your last and first name, and then click **OK**.

### Renaming and Creating Notebook Sections

A new OneNote notebook contains a single section named Untitled Section. To better identify the sections in the notebook, each should be given a unique name. By doing so, locating existing information and storing new information appropriately will be easier. You will now rename the Untitled Section in your new notebook and add new sections with appropriate names to support the information Mr. Cheney plans to collect.

### sp02.21 **To Rename and Create a Notebook Section**

a. If necessary, open the **sp01ws02Notebook_LastFirst** file from your RBGC Records - First Last folder on your OneDrive for Business account.

b. Right-click on **Untitled Section**, and then click **Rename**.

c. In the Section Name dialog box, type Pro Shop and then click **OK**.

d. On the INSERT tab, in the Notebook group, click **New Section**.

e. In the Section Name dialog box, type Bistro and then click **OK**.

f. On the INSERT tab, in the Notebook group, click **New Section**.

g. In the Section Name dialog box, type Putts for Paws and then click **OK**.

---

**SIDE NOTE**

**Tab Colors**

Section tabs can be recolored by right-clicking the section tab, clicking Section Color, and then selecting the desired color.

---

### Creating Page Content

Within each section in a notebook, at least one page exists. Content can be added anywhere on the page. OneNote Online allows for the insertion of formatted text, tags, tables, pictures, clip art, and links. Additional content can be added using the OneNote desktop application. You will now add some initial content to the Red Bluff Golf Club notebook.

### sp02.22 **To Create Page Content**

a. If necessary, open the **sp01ws02Notebook_LastFirst** file from your RBGC Records - First Last folder on your OneDrive for Business account.

b. Click the **Pro Shop** section tab, type General Thoughts, and then press Enter.

c. Type How can we promote lessons with golf pro John Schilling more?

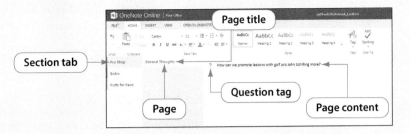

**Figure 16**   OneNote Online

d.   On the HOME tab, in the Tags group, click **Tag**, and then click **Question**.

e.   Click **FILE**, and then click **Exit**.

---

**REAL WORLD ADVICE**   **Tagging Page Content**

Tagging content in your pages makes it easy to visually identify content of importance within the notes. OneNote also supports searching notebook content based on tags, which can make it easier to locate content in larger notebooks.

---

**QUICK REFERENCE**   **Available Content Tags**

The available content tags in OneNote are To Do, Important, Question, Remember for later, Definition, Highlight, Contact, Address, Phone number, website to visit, Idea, Password, Critical, Project A, Project B, Movie to see, Book to read, Music to listen to, Source for article, Remember for blog, Discuss with <Person A>, Discuss with <Person B>, Discuss with manager, Send in email, Schedule meeting, Call back, To Do priority 1, To Do priority 2, and Client request.

---

## Create a Survey in Excel Online

A **survey** is a special feature of Excel Online that allows for the generation of a form with questions that can be distributed for completion with the results automatically stored in an Excel workbook. You can add a survey to an existing Excel workbook or you can create a new workbook to collect the survey results using the Excel survey option for new documents on OneDrive for Business.

Each question has associated text displayed to the end user completing the form and a type associated with the question that controls the information that can be entered in the field. At any point, the survey can be previewed or edited. Once complete, the survey can be shared with others for completion and collected results can be viewed in the workbook stored in SharePoint or OneDrive for Business.

### Creating a New Excel Survey

The fastest method to create a new Excel survey is by selecting the Excel survey option from the Create a new file callout from the new document button in any folder on your OneDrive for Business account. When creating the file, you will be prompted only for a file name and the new workbook will be saved in the current folder on the drive. When the file opens, the Edit Survey dialog box will be presented for editing the survey title, description, and creating questions.

Mr. Cheney wants to survey the Red Bluff Golf Course & Pro Shop employees regarding some potential changes in the operations. You will now create a new survey to gather the needed responses.

### sp02.23 To Create a New Excel Survey

a. If necessary, navigate to the **RBGC Records - First Last** folder in your OneDrive for Business account.

b. Click **new document**, and then click **Excel survey**.

c. In the Create a new document dialog box, type sp01ws02Survey_LastFirst and then click **OK**.

d. In the Edit Survey dialog box, click **Enter a title for your survey here**, and then type Proposed Operational Changes.

e. Click **Enter a description for your survey here**, and then type Please provide your opinion on the proposed operational changes at the Red Bluff Golf Course and Pro Shop.

f. Click **Enter your first question here**, click the **Question** box in the EDIT QUESTION callout, and then type To manage expenses, we are considering closing the Pro Shop one day a week. Which day do you feel is the best option if this change is adopted?

g. Click the **Response Type** box, and then click **Choice**.

h. Click to check the **Required** box.

i. Click the **Choices** box, and then type Sunday, Monday, Tuesday, Wednesday, Thursday, Friday, and Saturday, pressing Enter between each.

j. Click **Done**.

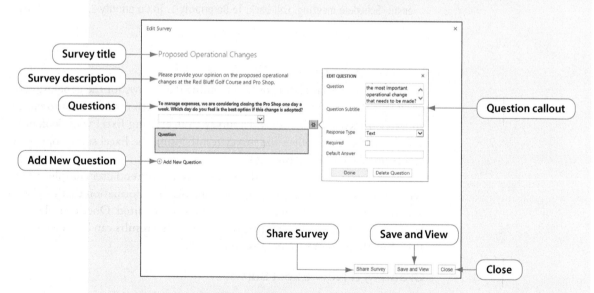

**Figure 17**   Edit Survey dialog box

k. Click **Add New Question**, then click the **Question** box, type In your opinion, what is the most important operational change that needs to be made?, and then click **Done**.

l. Leave the Edit Survey dialog box open for the next exercise.

> **Troubleshooting**
> If the file must be closed at this point, click Close on the Edit Survey dialog box, then click Save in the Unsaved Changes dialog box, and then Exit the Excel Online.

| QUICK REFERENCE | Question Response Types |
|---|---|

- Text—used for short responses
- Paragraph Text—used for multiline responses
- Number
- Date
- Time
- Yes/No
- Choice—allows user to select from a list of choices

## Previewing a Survey

Before distributing the survey, it is good practice to preview and test the form. Doing so provides an opportunity to make changes to answer types, correct spelling errors, and ensure that nothing was overlooked during the initial creation process. You will now preview and test the survey created for Mr. Cheney.

### sp02.24 To Preview a Survey

a. If necessary, reopen the **sp01ws02Survey_LastFirst** file from the RBGC Records - First Last folder on your OneDrive for Business account.

> **Troubleshooting**
> If you closed the file after the last activity, click EDIT WORKBOOK, and then click Edit in Excel Online to change the workbook view. Then on the HOME tab, in the Tables group, click Survey, and then click Edit Survey.

b. In the Edit Survey dialog box, click **Save and View**.

c. Click **Thursday**.

d. Click in the second question box, type Increase coverage for events and tournaments., and then click **Submit**.

e. Click **Close**.

## Editing a Survey

If changes to the survey content are required or additional questions need to be added after the initial creation process, Excel Online supports editing the survey to meet the current needs. In the review of the survey, Mr. Cheney realized that he had not asked an important question and wants you to add it to the survey. You will now edit the survey to include the missing question.

**To Edit an Excel Survey**

a. If necessary, reopen the **sp01ws02Survey_LastFirst** file from the RBGC Records - First Last folder on your OneDrive for Business account.

> **Troubleshooting**
> If you closed the file after the last activity, click EDIT WORKBOOK, and then click Edit in Excel Online to change the workbook view.

b. On the HOME tab, in the Tables group, click **Survey**, and then click **Edit Survey**.

c. In the Edit Survey dialog box, click **Add New Question**, then click the **Question** box, and then type Would you be interested in serving on a committee to review the survey results?

d. Click the **Question Subtitle** box, and then type Contact Mr. Cheney directly if interested.

e. Click the **Response Type** box, click **Yes/No**, click **Required**, and then click **Done**.

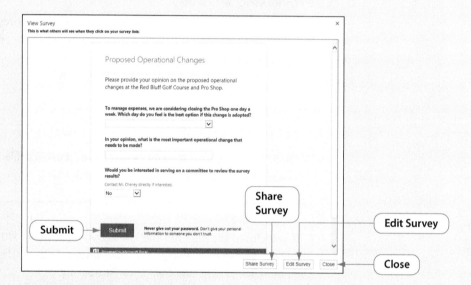

**Figure 18** View Survey dialog box

f. Click **Save and View**, and then click **Close**.

### Sharing a Survey

Once the survey is developed, the form needs to be made available to the people whose responses are needed. The **Share Survey** feature creates a link providing access to a web form without giving the end users access to the collected results or options to edit the survey in Excel Online. You will now share the completed survey with your instructor.

### sp02.26 To Share an Excel Survey

a. If necessary, reopen the **sp01ws02Survey_LastFirst** file from the RBGC Records - First Last folder on your OneDrive for Business account.

> **Troubleshooting**
>
> If you closed the file after the last activity, click EDIT WORKBOOK, and then click Edit in Excel Online to change the workbook view.

b. On the HOME tab, in the Tables group, click **Survey**, and then click **Share Survey**.

**Figure 19**  Share Survey dialog box

c. Right-click the link in the Share Survey dialog box, click **Copy**, and then click **Close**.

d. If instructed to do so, use your e-mail account to send the link to your instructor. Right-click in the body of the message, and then click **Paste**. Add an appropriate subject line and message body, and then click **Send**.

---

**REAL WORLD ADVICE**  **Collecting Survey Responses from People Outside Your Organization**

The Share Survey feature of the Excel Survey provides a link that can be shared with anyone for completion of the survey. This includes people outside of your organization. The results are automatically stored in the Excel workbook file in your OneDrive for Business account.

---

### Viewing Survey Responses

As respondents complete the survey online, the results are stored in the Excel workbook where the survey was created. To view the results, simply open the workbook using Excel Online. Each question is represented by a column heading with response values listed below each heading. You will now view the results received from the survey.

**To View Survey Responses**

a. If necessary, reopen the **sp01ws02Survey_LastFirst** file from the RBGC Records - First Last folder on your OneDrive for Business account.

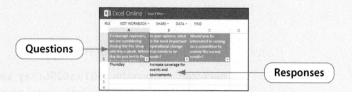

**Figure 20** View survey results

b. On the VIEW tab, in the Document Views group, click **Reading View**.

c. Click **FILE**, and then click **Exit**.

## Communicating on the Newsfeed

The SharePoint **newsfeed** is the default social networking component of SharePoint Server. From the newsfeed you can post ideas, comments, pictures, and more. You can also use the newsfeed to stay up to date on information shared by coworkers, items that you are following, and trending tags. The newsfeed features on the homepage of the sites using the team site template are automatically connected to the central newsfeed with updates posted to your newsfeed for sites that you follow.

In this next section, you will create various posts on the newsfeed, browse your personal newsfeed and newsfeeds on specific team sites, and manage newsfeed alerts and privacy settings.

### Create Newsfeed Posts

One of the key ways to get relevant content on the newsfeed is to create it. By starting conversations through original posts to your personal or team site newsfeed, others in the organization are notified of your thoughts and ideas and are encouraged to continue the conversation through replies, followings, or new posts of their own.

### Creating a Basic Newsfeed Post

A basic newsfeed post in SharePoint is text-based communication of your thoughts and ideas that are shared publicly with others in your organization. You will now access your personal newsfeed and create an initial post that promotes the need for volunteers to help with the Red Bluff Putts for Paws charity event.

**To Create a Newsfeed Post**

a. If necessary, open your web browser, navigate to your SharePoint Server URL, and then sign in with your user name and password.

b. On the top menu, click **Newsfeed**.

**Troubleshooting**

If your organization is using Yammer in place of the default SharePoint newsfeed, this section can be completed using a newsfeed on a team site designated by your instructor.

**Figure 21**   Start a conversation

c. Click the **Start a conversation** box, type Volunteers Needed! Let me know if you are available to help with the Red Bluff Putts for Paws charity event next week., and then click **Post**.

### Sending a Link to a Document from Your OneDrive for Business Account in a Post

When discussing ideas related to files stored in SharePoint or on your OneDrive for Business account, links to the source file can make it easier for other users to locate the content and add to the conversation. You will now add a post encouraging others to solicit corporate sponsors for the event using the letter created on your OneDrive for Business account.

### sp02.29 To Send a Link to a Document from Your OneDrive for Business Account in a Newsfeed Post

a. On the top menu, click **OneDrive**, and then navigate to your **Putts for Paws** subfolder.

b. On the **sp01ws02SponsorLetter_LastFirst** item, click **Open Menu** ⋯ .

c. Click the **URL** box, then right-click the selected text, and then click **Copy**.

d. Close the callout, and then in the top menu, click **Newsfeed**.

e. Click the **Start a conversation** box, and then type Do you know anyone who would like to be a corporate sponsor at the event? If so, share.

f.  Press the Spacebar, right-click at the insertion point, and then click **Paste**.

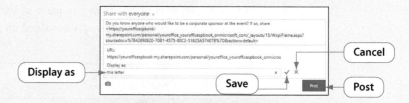

**Figure 22**  Display as box on post

g.  Click the **Display as** box, press Del, type this letter, and then click **Save** ✓.

> **Troubleshooting**
> If the Display as box does not appear, click in the URL pasted in the post.

h.  Press the Spacebar, type with them., and then click **Post**.

### Including a Picture in a Post

Including pictures in posts can make them stand out in the newsfeed. You will now post an invitation to the golfers in your organization to participate in the tournament and use the Red Bluff Golf Course logo to increase visibility of the post in the feed.

### sp02.30 To Insert a Picture in a Post

a.  If necessary, open your web browser and navigate to the SharePoint Newsfeed.

b.  Click the **Start a conversation** box, and then type Calling all golfers! Sign up today for the Red Bluff Putts for Paws tournament event.

c.  Click **Picture** 📷.

d.  In the Choose a picture dialog box, click **Browse**, and then navigate to your student data files.

e.  Click **sp01ws02GolfLogo**, click **Open**, and then click **Upload**.

f.  Click **Post**.

### Including Mentions and Tags in Posts

A **mention** in a newsfeed post references another user through the use of the @ symbol. By mentioning other users in a post, your post is shown in their newsfeed as an update.

Adding a tag to a newsfeed post uses the # symbol. Tags should be descriptive, but cannot include spaces. For multiple word phrases, simply remove the spaces in between the words. The newsfeed will also suggest tags based on ones used previously. Using the same tags as others in your organization makes posts visible to those users following the topic already.

You will now add a post to your newsfeed that mentions your instructor and uses a tag to personally invite him or her to the tournament event.

### sp02.31 To Include Mentions and Tags in Posts

a. If necessary, open your web browser and navigate to the SharePoint Newsfeed.

b. Click in the **Start a conversation** box, type @ followed by the first few characters of your instructor's name.

**Figure 23**   Mentions

c. When shown, click your instructor's name in the list, press the Spacebar, and then type Will you be joining a team for the #PuttsForPaws tournament this year?

d. Click **Post**.

### Browse the Newsfeed

In addition to being a tool for sharing information with colleagues throughout the organization, the newsfeed can serve as a source of information, delivering access to conversations that may otherwise be unavailable. Following people, documents, sites, or tags is a way to stay informed about the information most important to you. Additionally, the newsfeed has a search tool for browsing conversations by keywords or phrases.

As part of team sites, the newsfeed can manage conversations among team members. Items posted to a team site newsfeed are available to all members of the site.

### Browsing Your Personal Newsfeed

The SharePoint Newsfeed contains five default views: Following, Everyone, Mentions, Activities, and Likes. The default view of the newsfeed is Following, which shows the posts that have the most relevance to you based on tags, mentions, or your involvement in the conversation. The Everyone view contains all publicly available conversations started by people within your organization, whether or not you are following them.

You will now explore the various views of your personal newsfeed.

**To Explore the Personal Newsfeed**

a. If necessary, open your web browser and navigate to the SharePoint Newsfeed.

b. Click **Everyone**, and then click **Mentions**.

c. Click **Click for additional options** ⋯, and then click **Activities**.

d. Click **Click for additional options** ⋯, and then click **Likes**.

e. Click **Following**.

| QUICK REFERENCE | Following View of the Newsfeed |
|---|---|

The following types of information are presented in the Following view of the newsfeed:

- New conversations from those you currently follow
- Replies to your conversation posts
- Updates about the activities of people you are following
- Updates about the documents you are following
- Posts that contain a tag you are following

## Following People and Sites

**Following** people or sites subscribes you to updates and postings in your newsfeed related to those items. In order to get updates from all users discussing the upcoming tournament using the PuttsForPaws tag, you will now follow the tag from your newsfeed.

sp02.33 **To Follow People and Sites**

a. If necessary, open your web browser and navigate to the SharePoint Newsfeed.

b. On the **Following** view, locate your earlier post that included the **#PuttsForPaws** tag.

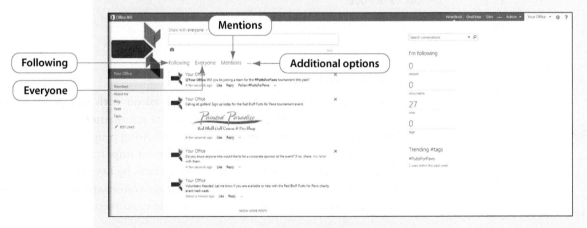

**Figure 24** Following view

c. Below the post, click **Follow #PuttsForPaws**.

Following people, sites, or documents will produce updates in your newsfeed when any of those items change. It is not necessary to follow everything, but this feature can ensure that you are notified of important changes as they occur. If the newsfeed gets too crowded, simply unfollow items of lesser importance.

## Update Your Newsfeed Settings

**Newsfeed settings** control tags that you are following, e-mail notifications related to your newsfeed, whether others see the people you are following and who are following you when viewing your profile, and which activities are shared in the newsfeed. Newsfeed settings are associated with your user profile and are updated in the About me section of SharePoint.

### Receiving E-mail Notifications

E-mail notifications can keep you informed when activity directly related to you occurs in the newsfeed. Although the additional notification can reduce the possibility of missing a notification on the newsfeed, too many notifications can clutter or fill your inbox. You will now set e-mail notification options on your newsfeed to limit notifications to those things that require the greatest attention.

### sp02.34 To Modify Newsfeed Settings

a. If necessary, open your web browser and navigate to the SharePoint Newsfeed.

b. Click your name on the top menu, and then click **About me**.

c. Click **edit your profile**, click **Click for additional options** ⋯ , and then click **Newsfeed Settings**.

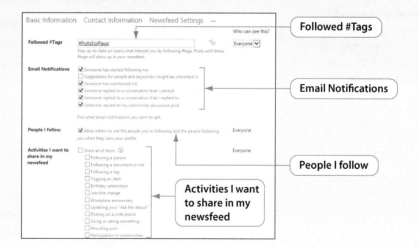

Figure 25   Newsfeed Settings

d. Click to uncheck **Suggestions for people and keywords I might be interested in**.

e. Click **Save all and close**, and then click **OK**.

**QUICK REFERENCE** | E-mail Notifications

E-mail notifications can be sent for the following newsfeed events:

- Someone has started following me
- Suggestions for people and keywords I might be interested in
- Someone has mentioned me
- Someone replied to a conversation that I started
- Someone replied to a conversation that I replied to
- Someone replied to my community discussion post

### Adjusting Privacy Settings

A wide variety of activities can be shared through the SharePoint newsfeed with other users in the organization. By sharing certain activities, you can encourage additional conversation about the shared information, whether that is helping others discover new connections or tags or simply reminding them of your birthday or workplace anniversary. You will now update your privacy settings to notify others when you follow a tag or update your "Ask Me About" profile settings.

**sp02.35 To Adjust Privacy Settings**

a.  If necessary, open your web browser and navigate to the SharePoint Newsfeed.

b.  Click your name on the top menu, and then click **About me**.

c.  Click **edit your profile**, click **Click for additional options** ⋯ , and then click **Newsfeed Settings**.

d.  Click **Following a tag**, and then click **Updating your "Ask Me About"**

e.  Click **Save all and close**, and then click **OK**.

**SIDE NOTE**

**Administrator Control**

Your system administrator decides which activities will appear in this list. There may be additional activities that show in your profile.

**QUICK REFERENCE** | Activities that Can Be Shared or Hidden

- Following a person
- Following a document or site
- Following a tag
- Tagging an item
- Birthday celebration
- Job title change

- Workplace anniversary
- Updating your "Ask Me About"
- Posting on a note board
- Liking or rating something
- New blog post
- Participation in communities

**CONSIDER THIS** | Personal Privacy

What is a comfortable level of privacy at work? What information are you willing to share with others? Are there differences in your comfort level for settings on your organization SharePoint Server Newsfeed versus other social networks such as Facebook?

## Concept Check

1. How can tags and notes be used to organize files on your OneDrive for Business account?

2. What is the difference between inserting a picture and inserting clip art images in Word Online?

3. What types of charts can be created in Excel Online?

4. What is meant by the terms themes and variants in PowerPoint Online?

5. How are notebooks organized using OneNote Online?

6. What is an Excel Survey?

7. What is a mention and how is it designated in SharePoint newsfeed posts?

8. What newsfeed events can be used to trigger e-mail notifications?

## Key Terms

Bookmarklet 46
Clip Art 51
Cloud storage 42
Comments 60
Editing view 50
Excel Online 54
Followed Documents 42
Following 72
Hierarchal structure 43
Mention 71
Newsfeed 68

Newsfeed settings 73
Note 45
Notes (PowerPoint Online) 60
Notes pane 60
Office Online 50
OneDrive for Business 42
OneNote Online 61
Open in Word 50
Picture 51
PowerPoint Online 56

Reading view 50
Share Survey 67
Shared with Me 42
Slide layout 58
Slide Show view 56
Survey 63
Tag 45
Theme 57
Variant 57
Word Online 50

## Visual Summary

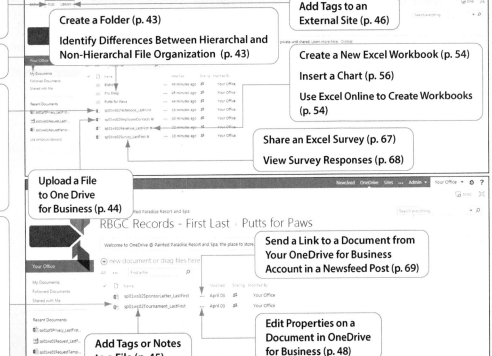

Set an Alert on a File in OneDrive for Business (p. 49)

Share a Folder with Other Users (p. 48)

Create a New Notebook (p. 62)

Rename and Create a Notebook Section (p. 62)

Create Page Content (p. 62)

Use OneNote Online to Create a Notebook (p. 61)

Create a New Word Document (p. 51)

Insert Images and Clip Art (p. 51)

Insert Comments Using Reading View (p. 52)

Print from and Exit Word Online (p. 53)

Use Word Online to Create Documents (p. 50)

Create a Folder (p. 43)

Identify Differences Between Hierarchal and Non-Hierarchal File Organization (p. 43)

Upload a File to One Drive for Business (p. 44)

Add Tags or Notes to a File (p. 45)

Add Tags to an External Site (p. 46)

Create a New Excel Workbook (p. 54)

Insert a Chart (p. 56)

Use Excel Online to Create Workbooks (p. 54)

Share an Excel Survey (p. 67)

View Survey Responses (p. 68)

Send a Link to a Document from Your OneDrive for Business Account in a Newsfeed Post (p. 69)

Edit Properties on a Document in OneDrive for Business (p. 48)

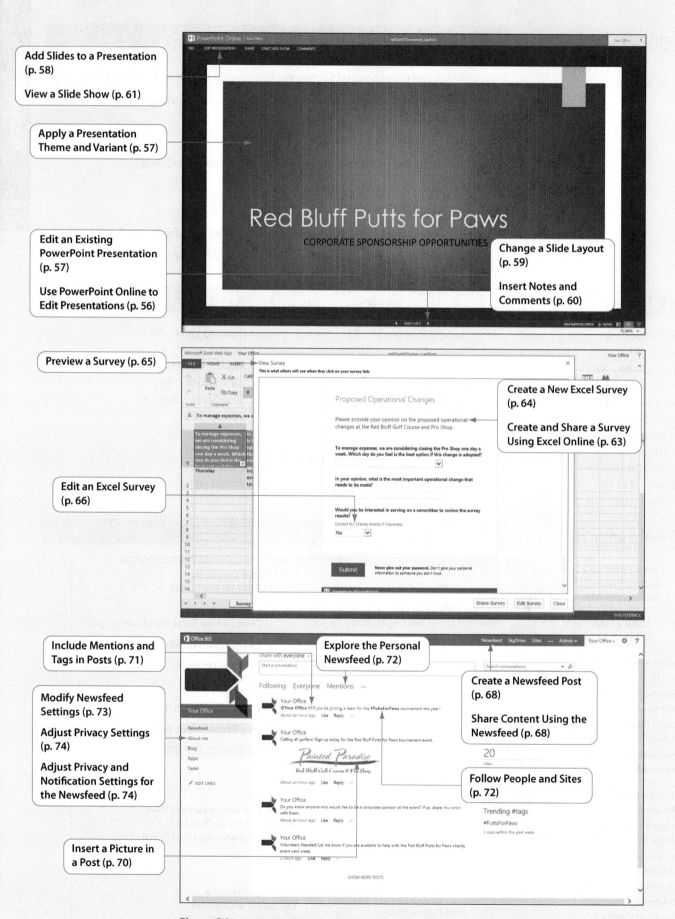

**Add Slides to a Presentation** (p. 58)

**View a Slide Show** (p. 61)

**Apply a Presentation Theme and Variant** (p. 57)

**Edit an Existing PowerPoint Presentation** (p. 57)

**Use PowerPoint Online to Edit Presentations** (p. 56)

**Change a Slide Layout** (p. 59)

**Insert Notes and Comments** (p. 60)

**Preview a Survey** (p. 65)

**Create a New Excel Survey** (p. 64)

**Create and Share a Survey Using Excel Online** (p. 63)

**Edit an Excel Survey** (p. 66)

**Include Mentions and Tags in Posts** (p. 71)

**Explore the Personal Newsfeed** (p. 72)

**Create a Newsfeed Post** (p. 68)

**Modify Newsfeed Settings** (p. 73)

**Share Content Using the Newsfeed** (p. 68)

**Adjust Privacy Settings** (p. 74)

**Adjust Privacy and Notification Settings for the Newsfeed** (p. 74)

**Follow People and Sites** (p. 72)

**Insert a Picture in a Post** (p. 70)

**Figure 26** Collaborating through sites, OneDrive, and Newsfeed

**Student data file needed:**

 None

**You will create a new shared folder named:**

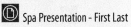 Spa Presentation - First Last

**You will save your file as:**

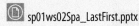 sp01ws02Spa_LastFirst.pptx

### Turquoise Oasis Spa Presentation

Sales & Marketing

Meda Rodate, Manager of the Turquoise Oasis Spa, has asked you to create a PowerPoint presentation advertising the spa's massage staff and services using PowerPoint Online, saving the file in a shared folder on your OneDrive for Business account.

a. Start your web browser, navigate to your OneDrive for Business account, and then sign in using your user name and password.

b. On the FILES tab, in the New group, click **New Folder**.

c. In the **Name** box, type Spa Presentation - First Last using your first and last name, and then click **Save**.

d. On the **Spa Presentation - First Last** folder, click **Open Menu** ⋯ , and then click **SHARE**.

e. In the **Enter names, email addresses, or 'Everyone'.** box, type your instructor's email address and then click **Share**.

f. Click **Spa Presentation - First Last**.

g. Click **new document**, and then click **PowerPoint presentation**.

h. In the **Document Name** box, type sp01ws02Spa_LastFirst using your last and first name, and then click **OK**.

i. On the DESIGN tab, in the Themes group, click **More Themes**, and then click **Celestial**.

j. On the DESIGN tab in the Variants group, click **Variant 3**.

k. Click **CLICK TO ADD TITLE**, and then type Turquoise Oasis Spa.

l. Click **CLICK TO ADD SUBTITLE**, and then type A passion for helping people relax.

m. On the HOME tab, in the Slides group, click **New Slide**, click **Two Content**, and then click **Add Slide**.

n. Click **CLICK TO ADD TITLE**, and then type Massage Therapists.

o. Click in the first content placeholder, type Pat Bruner, and then press Enter.

p. Type the following names pressing Enter between each: Jason Chambers, Christy Istas, Kendra Mault, Susan Mullin, and Jason Niese.

q. Click in the second content placeholder, and then on the INSERT tab, in the Images group, click **Clip Art**.

r. In the search box, type massage, and then press Enter.

s. Click the first image, and then click **Insert**.

t. On the HOME tab, in the Slides group, click **New Slide**, click **Title Slide**, and then click **Add Slide**.

u. Click **CLICK TO ADD TITLE**, and then type Schedule Today.

v. Click **CLICK TO ADD SUBTITLE**, and then type Call to set an appointment.

w. Click **FILE**, and then click **Exit**.

**Student data file needed:**
None

**You will save your file as:**
sp01ps1Survey_LastFirst.xlsx

## Coffee Shop Survey

Research & Development

Paul Medina, manager of Terra Cotta Brew, is exploring changes to the coffee shop menu and would like to survey employees and customers across the Painted Paradise Golf Resort and Spa before making final decisions on the new offerings. He has asked you to create a survey using Excel Online, save the survey on your OneDrive for Business account, and provide a link that he can share with others to complete the survey.

a. Start your web browser, navigate to your OneDrive for Business account, and sign in using your user name and password.

b. In a folder of your choosing, create a new **Excel survey**, named sp01ps1Survey_LastFirst using your last and first name.

c. Edit the survey **title**, and then type Terra Cotta Brew Menu Options.

d. Edit the survey **description**, and then type We want your feedback on possible changes to our menu at Terra Cotta Brew.

e. Enter the first question using the text How often do you visit Terra Cotta Brew?, and the **Choice** response type with the following choices: Once a week, Once a day, Two or more times a day, Less than once a week.

f. Enter a second question using the text If we began serving breakfast sandwiches, would you be likely to visit more?, and the **Yes/No** response type.

g. Enter a third question using the text What item would you most like to see added to our menu? and the **Text** response type.

h. Share the survey with your instructor via e-mail.

**Student data file needed:**
None

**You will save your file as:**
sp01pf1Notebook_LastFirst

## Computer Concepts Notebook

Information Technology

You quickly realized the benefits to storing and organizing notes in OneNote and decided that you could benefit from setting up a new notebook for your computer class this semester to collect notes and ideas related to SharePoint and the other concepts you are learning. You will create a new notebook in your OneDrive for Business account with sections for each of the main topic areas covered in your course and add notes related to SharePoint Server 2013.

a. Start your web browser, navigate to your OneDrive for Business account, and sign in using your user name and password.

b. In a folder of your choosing, create a new OneNote notebook named sp01pf1Notebook_ LastFirst using your last and first name.

c. Add sections to the notebook for all of the main topics to be covered in the course.

d. Create notes related to SharePoint Server 2013 in the appropriate sections.

e. Close the notebook and share the file with your instructor through your OneDrive for Business account.

## MODULE CAPSTONE

**More Practice 1**

**Student data file needed:**

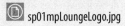 sp01mpLoungeLogo.jpg

**You will save your site as:**

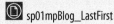 sp01mpBlog_LastFirst

### Create an Events Blog

General
Business

Will Diaz, manager of the Silver Moon Lounge, thinks that a blog will be useful for promoting the events and happenings at the lounge. He has asked you to set up the blog and create an initial post telling everyone to look for upcoming events to be posted soon.

a. Start your web browser, and then navigate and sign in to the SharePoint Team Site provided by your instructor.

b. Click **Site Contents**, and then click **new subsite**.

c. In the **Title** box, type Silver Moon Events, and then in the **URL name** box, type sp01mpBlog_LastFirst.

d. Under the Template Selection section, on the Collaboration tab, click **Blog**.

e. Under Display this site on the Quick Launch of the parent site?, click **Yes**.

f. Under Use the top link bar from the parent site?, click **Yes**.

g. Click **Create**.

h. Click **Settings** ⚙, and then click **Site settings**.

i. Under the Look and Feel heading, click **Title, description, and logo**.

j. Under the Insert Logo heading, click **FROM COMPUTER**, navigate to your Student Data Files, and then click **sp01mpLoungeLogo**.

k. Click **Open**, click **OK**, and then click **OK**.

l. On the Quick Launch, click **Home**.

m. In the Blog tools navigation, click **Manage posts**.

n. On the **Welcome to my blog!** item, click **Edit** 📝.

o. In the **Title** box, select the text, press [Del], and then type Check here for upcoming event information!

p. In the **Body** box, select the text, press [Del], type This blog will be regularly updated with information about upcoming events at the Silver Moon Lounge and pictures from our past events., press [Enter], and then type Bookmark the page to stay informed!

q. If necessary, under the Category heading, click **Events**, and then click **Add**.

r. Click **Publish**, and then on the Quick Launch, click **Home**.

**Student data file needed:**

 None

**You will save your notebook file as:**

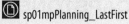 sp01mpPlanning_LastFirst

### Event Planning Notes

Production & Operations

Patti Rochelle, the Corporate Event Planner at Painted Paradise Golf Resort & Spa, thinks that a OneNote notebook in a shared OneDrive folder would be a great way to keep up with all of the details related to the various events managed by her department. She has asked that you create a notebook with sections for each of the conference spaces and help her set up a page for one of the upcoming events.

a. Start your web browser, navigate to your OneDrive for Business account, and sign in using your user name and password.

b. Click the **FILES** tab, and in the New group, click **New Folder**.

c. In the **Name** box, type Planning Notes - First Last using your first and last name, and then click **Save**.

d. Click **Planning Notes - First Last**, click **new document**, and then click **OneNote notebook**.

e. In the **Document Name** box, type sp01mpPlanning_LastFirst using your last and first name, and then click **OK**.

f. Right-click the **Untitled Section** tab, and then click **Rename**.

g. Click in the **Enter a section name** box, select the text, press ⌷Del⌷, type The Musica Room, and then click **OK**.

h. On the INSERT tab, in the Notebook group, click **New Section**.

i. In the **Enter a section name** box, type The Eldorado Room and then click **OK**.

j. On the INSERT tab, in the Notebook group, click **New Section**.

k. In the **Enter a section name** box, type The Pueblo Room and then click **OK**.

l. Click **Untitled Page** to the right of **The Musica Room**, and type Upcoming Events.

m. Click below the page title, and then type August 18, 2015: Smith-Donahue Wedding.

n. Click **FILE**, click **Share**, and then click **Share with People**.

o. Click the **Enter names, email addresses, or 'Everyone'.** box, type your instructor's email address, and then click **Share**.

**Student data file needed:**

 None

**You will create the following custom lists:**

 Anna Kachina's Jewelry

Painted Paradise Linens

Indigo5 Products

Turquoise Oasis Spa Products

### Inventory Lists for Painted Treasures

Production & Operations

Susan Brock, the Manager of the Painted Treasures Gift Shop, would like to add several custom lists to the Painted Treasures team site for keeping track of inventory levels of the various products available in the shop. Using the Painted Treasures team site created in Workshop 1, you will add custom lists for Anna Kachina's jewelry, Painted Paradise linens, Indigo5 products, and Turquoise Oasis Spa products available in the shop.

a. Start your web browser; navigate and sign in to the Painted Treasures Team Site created in Workshop 1.

b. Add four **Custom List** apps to the site with the following names: Anna Kachina's Jewelry, Painted Paradise Linens, Indigo5 Products, and Turquoise Oasis Spa Products.

c. Add the following items to the **Turquoise Oasis Spa Products** list: New Mexico Mud Mask, Turquoise Oasis Exfoliating Sponge, Turquoise Oasis Moisturizing Cream, Geranium Rose Bath Salts, Cilantro Foot Bath Salts, and Avocado Foot Care Cream.

d. Edit the List Settings for **Anna Kachina's Jewelry**, and create two additional columns with **Currency** type, named Cost, and Retail Price.

e. Edit the Quick Launch links to order the four custom lists alphabetically between the Home and Notebook links for the team site.

## Problem Solve 2

**Student data file needed:**

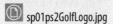 sp01ps2GolfLogo.jpg

**You will save your file as:**

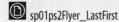 sp01ps2Flyer_LastFirst

### Document Sharing on the Newsfeed

Sales & Marketing

Using the team site that you created for Red Bluff Golf Course in Workshop 1, you will create a marketing flyer for the upcoming Red Bluff Putts for Paws charity tournament event in the team site document library and then share a link to the flyer through a newsfeed post with others in your organization.

a. Start your web browser; navigate and sign in to the Red Bluff Golf Course team site you created in Workshop 1.

b. In the Documents library, create a new **Word document** named sp01ps2Flyer_LastFirst.

c. Design a flyer for the Red Bluff Putts for Paws charity tournament event that includes the event title, an appropriate clip art image, and the **sp01ps2GolfLogo** file from your Student Data files.

d. Include the following details on the flyer: Silent Auction, Teams Forming Now, Reception, and Corporate Sponsorship Opportunities Available.

e. Modify the placement and formatting of the document to fit the content to a single page.

f. Create a newsfeed post on the team site newsfeed that includes an announcement that the flyer is available with a link to the document in the Documents library.

## Perform 1: Perform in Your Life

**Student data file needed:**

 None

**You will save your file as:**

sp01pf1Privacy_LastFirst

### A Personal Level of Privacy

Information Technology

The Newsfeed feature of SharePoint allows for the sharing of information with others in your organization; however, everyone has their own personal levels of desired privacy. Based on your personal desires for sharing information with others, you will set the appropriate options to show or hide each of the "Activities I want to share in my newsfeed" items in the Newsfeed Settings. You will then create a new Word document to include a screen clipping of this section of the Newsfeed Settings page and a brief explanation for each of your choices in the document. Once complete, you will upload the document to your OneDrive for Business storage location and share the file with your instructor.

a. Start your web browser, navigate and sign in to your SharePoint account.

b. Based on your personal desires for sharing information with others, set the appropriate options to show or hide each of the "Activities I want to share in my newsfeed" items in the Newsfeed Settings.

c. Using your Word desktop app, create a new document named **sp01pf1Privacy_LastFirst** using your last and first name and insert a screen clipping of the "Activities I want to share in my newsfeed" section of your Newsfeed Settings page.

d. For each of the activities in the list, identify the choice made and a brief explanation for the choice.

e. Save and upload the file to your OneDrive for Business storage.

f. Share the file on your OneDrive with your instructor.

## Perform 2: Perform in Your Career

**Student data file needed:**

 None

**You will save your file as:**

 sp01pf2Survey_LastFirst

### Customer Experience Survey

Research & Development

You are the manager for a local restaurant and are committed to providing high quality food and service to your patrons. Although you try to personally visit each table during the dining experience and ask for feedback on the meal and service, you feel that often the feedback is limited. As a result, you want to begin collecting formal survey results on all aspects of the dining experience through an online survey. To do so, you will create an Excel survey to collect this valuable customer feedback.

a. Start your web browser, navigate to your OneDrive for Business account, and then sign in using your user name and password.

b. Create a new **Excel survey** file named **sp01pf2Survey_LastFirst** using your last and first name.

c. Add an appropriate title and description to the survey.

d. Create at least five questions using a variety of response types, including at least one **Choice** type with three or more choices of response.

e. Preview and share the survey with your instructor.

## Perform 3: Perform in Your Team

**Student data file needed:**

 None

**You will save your file as:**

 sp01pf3ComputerClub_LastFirst

### Commenting on Shared Documents

General Business

You have been asked by the campus computer club to create a flyer to promote its upcoming workshop on the benefits of Cloud storage using OneDrive for Business. Using Word Online, design a flyer that includes the following details and share that flyer with at least one classmate for feedback. Reply to the comments made by your classmate with additional comments of your own and make any adjustments that you feel are appropriate based on the suggestions.

a. Start your web browser, navigate to your OneDrive for Business account, and then sign in using your user name and password.

b. Create a new **Word document** file named sp01pf3ComputerClub_LastFirst using your last and first name.

c. Using Word Online, design a flyer for a workshop to be held next Wednesday on the benefits of Cloud storage using OneDrive for Business.

d. Include at least one clip art image in the flyer and make adjustments to the formatting of text and images to fit the content on a single page.

e. Share the file with a classmate for feedback, asking him or her to add comments in the Reading view of the document.

f. Reply and address any comments added to the file and save changes.

## Perform 4: How Others Perform

**Student data file needed:**

 sp01pf4Structure.docx

**You will save your file as:**

 sp01pf4Visualization_LastFirst

### Improving Internal Communication

Human Resources

A college adopting SharePoint to improve internal communication across the various departments created a site collection that mirrored the organizational structure. After having this site collection in place for a while, it has been observed that information in the individual sites is being used by the respective departments, but it has done little to improve communication among departments. Consider ways that the site collection could be reorganized to reflect college-level functions and meet the expressed communication goals. Create a visualization of the revised site collection using Microsoft Word.

a. Open the **sp01pf4Structure** file from your Student Data Files and review the current site structure.

b. Consider the interdepartmental communication processes that exist in a college environment based on the current structure and outline a reorganization of the site collection that will better meet the communication needs of the organization.

c. Using Word 2013, create a SmartArt object that illustrates the proposed revisions to the site collection. Save the document as sp01pf4Visualization_LastFirst.

d. Upload the completed file to your OneDrive for Business account and share the file with your instructor.

# Glossary

## A

**App** refers to a list, library, or other configurable component for creating or maintaining site content

## B

**blog template** allows for posting ideas with inherent commenting tools for site visitor use

**bookmarklet** a link that is added to the Web browser's favorites or bookmarks toolbar to run a script that sends information to sites on the Internet

## C

**calendar app** provides a central location for listing events and activities that impact the team as a whole or resources shared by team members

**child site (subsite)** the new site created from a parent site

**Clip Art** a searchable collection of royalty-free images provided by Microsoft for insertion in the document

**Cloud storage** the storage of data in an online location that is accessible across an Internet connection

**comments** a feedback feature that allows multiple users to discuss the file with direct connection to the related content

**community site template** a discussion-driven site where content can be searched, sorted, and rated

**custom list** can be created for any information that can be consistently represented by predetermined fields

## D

**discussion board** provides a threaded message board that is available to all members of the team without cluttering the team members' inbox with unnecessary e-mail messages

**disposition approval workflow** manages document expiration and retention by allowing participants to decide whether to retain or delete expired documents

**Document library** a place for storing documents or other files that you want to share

**document version history** a feature of SharePoint libraries that retains copies of previously saved versions of files stored in the library

## E

**Editing view** the view that allows for modification of file contents and use of the editing tools on the Ribbon

**Excel Online** provides the ability to work directly and collaboratively on Excel workbooks stored in OneDrive for Business or SharePoint sites

## F

**Followed Documents** OneDrive for Business link that provides quick access to files throughout your organization's SharePoint sites and libraries

**following** subscribes you to updates and postings in your newsfeed related to those items

**Form library** a place to manage business forms like status reports or purchase orders

**form template** applied to form libraries to consistently collect the data stored in the library

## G

**group** created with a unique name to represent multiple people, or individual users, within the organization

## H

**hierarchal structure** consists of folders and subfolders containing related files

## L

**library** a special purpose list that is used to store files and information about those files

**list** used to store and manage information, such as tasks or calendar events, organized into columns of information representing specific attributes of each item in the list

**logo** an image file placed in the upper left corner of the site pages to the left of the top link bar and above the Quick Launch

## M

**member** a user role in SharePoint that is typically granted contribute permission, allowing him or her to contribute content to existing lists and libraries and edit page content, but not to create additional lists and libraries or modify site structure or permissions

**mention** references another user in a newsfeed post

**Microsoft InfoPath** provides the technology for designing form templates that can be published to SharePoint Form Libraries, as well as the technology for filling out forms associated with the libraries in place on a SharePoint site

## N

**newsfeed** the social networking component of SharePoint Server

**Newsfeed settings** control tags that you are following, e-mail notifications related to your newsfeed, whether others see the people you are following and who is following you when viewing your profile, and which activities are shared in the newsfeed

**note** used to comment on pages, documents, and external sites

**notes (PowerPoint Online)** record content that is shared verbally, but not included on the displayed slide

**Notes pane** displays below the current slide in the Editing view of the presentation in PowerPoint Online

## O

**Office Online** the online companions to Word, Excel, PowerPoint, and OneNote

**OneDrive for Business** a cloud storage location, included in SharePoint 2013, for personal organization of work-related documents

**OneNote Online** provides access to electronic notebooks that make it easy to store, organize, and share a variety of content in a single location online

**Open in Word** opens the document in the Word desktop application, if installed on the computer, for full functionality and editing features

**owner** a user role in SharePoint that is typically granted full control permission, allowing him or her to create, edit, add, and delete content, lists, libraries, site structure, and permissions

## P

**parent site** the active site when a new site is created

**permissions** define the level of access that is granted to a site, page, list, library, or item

**picture** image file stored on your computer that can be uploaded for use in the document

**Picture library** a place to upload and share pictures

**PowerPoint Online** supports the viewing, editing, and printing of PowerPoint presentations from within the web browser

**project site template** brings all status, communication, and artifacts relevant to a project into one place

## Q

**Quick Launch** the left side menu area in a SharePoint site that provides access to all of the other content areas created by or available to the site template

## R

**Reading view** shows the document as it will appear in the full application or in print form, with options to print and share the document, to search for content, or to add or review comments

**Ribbon** the tabbed interface containing the Browse tab, core page control buttons, and other context-sensitive buttons and tabs depending on the page being viewed

## S

**Share Survey** creates a link providing access to a Web form, without giving the end users access to the collected results or options to edit the survey in Excel Online

**Shared with Me** OneDrive for Business link that provides access to any files that other users have shared with you from their OneDrive for Business accounts

**site collection** multiple related sites within SharePoint Server

**site template** preconfigured site options that include common lists and libraries related to the intended purpose of that site

**slide layout** designates the number, location, and related content association of placeholders on the slide

**Slide library** allows for the sharing of slides from Microsoft PowerPoint, or a compatible application, and provides special features for finding, managing, and reusing slides

**Slide Show view** displays the presentation full-screen, allowing presentation directly from the browser

**survey** a special feature of Excel Online that allows for the generation of a form with questions that can be distributed for completion, with the results automatically stored in an Excel workbook

## T

**tag** used to classify and remember pages, documents, or external sites in SharePoint

**team site template** contains basic components needed to immediately begin sharing documents, maintain a central team notebook, and create or organize information important to the team

**theme** provides a consistent look and feel to your SharePoint site by consistently applying fonts and colors throughout the site

**theme (PowerPoint Online)** provides a visual structure to the presentation, including colors, fonts, effects, background styles, and placeholder positioning

**three-state workflow** used to track items in a list or library

**top-level team site** the starting point for a site collection providing a site homepage, a shared document library, and a notebook

**top link bar** appears below the Ribbon, provides navigation to the homepage of the current site, and includes a search bar

**top menu** a menu at the very top of the page that provides access to various features of SharePoint, profile options, settings, and help features

## U

**user role** in SharePoint three basic roles exist: visitor, member, and owner

## V

**variant** provides alternative options for the base theme with modifications to colors, fonts, or effects

**view** applied to lists to show specific columns, to filter the results shown, and to apply sorts to the values entered

**visitor** a user role in SharePoint that is typically granted read-only access to information contained in the site

## W

**Wiki page library** an interconnected set of easily editable web pages, which can contain text, images, and Web parts

**Word Online** provides the core functionality of Microsoft Word for viewing, printing, and editing Word documents in the browser

**workflow** predefined sequence of tasks associated with items in libraries or lists

# Index